MW01147627

The 22 Laws of Category Design

The 22 Laws of Category Design
Copyright © 2023 Category Pirates

ISBN: Paperback 978-1-956934-57-1

Cover and interior designed by Zoe Norvell

The 22 Laws of Category Design

Name & Claim Your Niche,
Share Your POV, And Move
The World From Where It Is
To Somewhere Different

To the bold, the daring, the different—
this book is dedicated to you.

It's for those of you who refuse to fit into
molds, who question the status quo, and
who risk it all to design new categories
rather than competing in old ones. May your
courage remain unyielding, your ideas always
forward-looking, and your impact truly
legendary. Because as Steve Jobs once said,
only those crazy enough to think they can
change the world, are the ones who do.

—The Category Pirates

Table of Contents

Part 3: Product

Part 4: Company

Introduction

It's weird to start a book by telling you that you should not read this book, but that's exactly what we're going to do.

Let us explain.

We know that most people who buy business books don't actually read them. So the fact that your eyeballs are scrolling through these words honors us greatly. (Sincerely, thank you.) That said, we want to be very clear about what you can expect from this book.

Unlike most business books that try to appeal to as many people as possible, this book is (purposely) not for everyone.

Instead, it's for a very small percentage of business people.

We know that sounds nuts. We've written for major publishers in the past who told us to write for as broad of an audience as possible. (In case you haven't met us before, it's important you know that we have a healthy disrespect for conventional wisdom. Most business books are written by one, maybe two, people. This book is different. It's written by our writing band, called Category Pirates. You can learn more about each of us in our bios at the end of the book.)

Here's the thing: It's human nature to fit in, not stand out.

If you prefer the former, this book is not for you.

We love and respect you, but you should put this book down and do something else. Why? Because everything we say in here will piss you off. You see, most people in business are *not* trying to use category design to create a new category that changes the future and generates exponential new value. Instead, many people in business are trying to "not get fired." Many people want to go to work, contribute, and go home. And people earn a wonderful living while running, optimizing, and improving a business or part of a business.

We respect all of that. The world really needs you. But we are not qualified to help you.

This book is for the small percentage of business people who have a *different* mind.

It's purpose-built for people who want to make an exponential difference, not be incrementally better.

We respect the people who do incremental improvements.

A bunch of incremental improvements, over an extended period of time, can be very powerful. Incremental improvement is just not what category design is about. And it's not what this book is about.

Category design is about the exponentially different. It's about creating different futures by creating new and different business categories.

Category design is not about competing. It's about creating.

This is an outlier concept in the business world, so here's a quick overview. Category design is a business discipline that helps companies earn the majority of the value created in a specific new or different category of products or services. (Primary research on category design in *Play Bigger*, the first category design book, shows that in technology categories, one company earns 76 percent of the total market cap value created.)

Category design involves educating the market about a new, often-ignored problem as well as a solution that you can provide.

It is often associated with a breakthrough product or service, a breakthrough business model, and big data about future category signals and demand shifts. Dominating a new category is not necessarily about being the first to market a product. It is about being the first company to have your definition of a problem and, therefore, the solution, tip at scale. For example, Apple did not create the mobile phone category (that accomplishment goes to Motorola). But Apple did redesign the category with a fresh point of view (POV) and a radically different product, the glass touch screen smartphone.

When category design is done successfully, you:

- Become known for a niche you own
- Attract a loyal following of high-spending Superconsumers
- Earn the majority of market value (76 percent)

In other words, you make it impossible for someone else to "do what you do." So, you become the Category King. And ultimately, you change the world *and* create exponentially more value for customers, employees, and stakeholders in the process.

In category design, it's winner takes all.

This is also what happens in modern technology-powered market categories. With the rise of the Internet, the mobile phone, the cloud, and now AI, every market category and every company is a tech company. This means non-tech industries and market categories will increasingly behave like native-tech ones. This means non-tech categories will likely evolve to exhibit tech-category economics over time.

Translation: One company wins big in each category.

But most marketers, entrepreneurs, creators, and investors spend their entire careers competing for only 24 percent of the value opportunity of a given category. They're not the Category King—and they don't even know it. As a result, they waste time and effort competing over demand instead of creating new demand in a category they dominate.

Legendary companies, and people with legendary careers, create new things. They don't fight over old things.

In a world where more and more legacy categories are becoming commoditized, being perceived as unique is the ultimate advantage. The perception of being irreplaceable is the moat to rule them all. If you don't start, invest in, or work for a category creator or category-designing company that creates net-new territory, you are making the unconscious decision to compete over a small sliver of someone else's plot of land.

Consciously or unconsciously, you are saying, "I don't want to be part of creating the future."

That's why this book is for the dreamers, innovators, and pirates who want to create massive *new* value. The "crazy" ones (hat tip to Steve). The people who are "stupid" enough to think their vision is possible. Our best guess is that less than 10 percent of CEOs, entrepreneurs, C-level executives, product developers, sales leaders, creators, and marketers will ever practice category design.

We also must tell you, if you're schooled in traditional growth, marketing, and startup thinking, much of this book will undermine what you've been taught. If that sounds upsetting, return the book or gift it to someone you consider "crazy." But if that sounds legendary, get ready to change your life. (We know this sounds absurd, but we know it to be true.)

This book is for those who want to continually reflect on category design so they can transform their thinking, actions, and outcomes.

Some books are read once, front to back, then put away because you just want the information. Some books have one interesting idea, repeated in different ways over two hundred pages. Some books have obvious insights you can easily recite but that don't really change your work, career, or life.

This book is 100 percent the opposite.

This book is meant to be read repeatedly, even if it's for five minutes a day.

Why? Because it's designed to read you, as much as you read it. Category design requires the unlearning of much of what you've been taught about strategy, marketing, and business. To unlearn, you have to commit to the daily transformation of turning your reflexive thinking into reflective thinking.

Unlearning is way harder than learning.

That's why certain chapters include several "thinking about thinking" exercises that we want you to set aside time to ask yourself. In order to unlock different outcomes in your life, you must change the way you think and change the way you act. But you must also change the way you feel. These questions are designed for you to ask yourself harder, deeper, and at times, scarier questions.

Changing how you think is hard. Changing your behavior is hard.

If you haven't changed your mind lately, how do you know you have one?

(inspired by Edward de Bono)

Take your time with these ideas and let them marinate to transform your brain. Let them steep into your bones so when you take action, you mean it.

Category Design is something you "learn," but it is more so something you "get."

This book is for every Luke or Leia Skywalker who needs a shot of Obi-Wan and a sip of Yoda in their life to challenge them, change them, and help them transform into a Jedi Master. And if you're a Category Design Sensei, a multi-time successful entrepreneur, executive, pirate, dreamer, or innovator, you know how steel sharpens steel.

Your first lesson: Everything is the way it is because somebody changed the way it was.

This book is meant to ignite that change, and you can read it in any sequence you want. We want you to read the table of contents, reflect on the dreams that excite you and the nightmares that scare you, then go to the precise chapter that helps you the most that day.

To help you navigate and find what you need most, the book is organized into four parts.

Part 1: Foundational Thinking. This section shares why category design can help you capture the lion's share of a market's economics and explains core category design frameworks.

Part 2: Category. This section dives deeper into how to design and dominate a category by recognizing a problem and creating a solution.

Part 3: Product. This section explains how to create a product that people want, love, and are willing to tell the world about.

Part 4: Company. This section explains how to set your company apart by creating the future and bringing others into that new and different future.

Most importantly, you'll find twenty-two core principles of category design—any one of which could unlock a million, billion, or even trillion-dollar outcome for you, your company, and your career.

This book will educate you on how to use category design to exit the fight for "demand capture" and enter the game of "demand creation." That means you stop fighting over old territory someone else owns and, instead, go on a mission to create net-new territories that don't exist in the world... *yet*. To make the most of the frameworks, strategies, and prompts in this book, you need a radical willingness to consider a different point of view about how to design a legendary business and career.

Consider this your warning:

- This book requires a ton of unlearning.
- A lot of smart people think the contents of this book are dumb.
- You might be called dumb if you start to implement the strategies inside this book.
- It's okay to put this book down and walk away.

If you're still reading, get ready to make an exponential difference.

Part 1

FOUNDATIONAL THINKING

Thinking About Thinking Is the Most Important Kind of Thinking

Expertise is the enemy of fresh thinking.

Category design is a game of thinking.

If you want to find success as a category designer, you have to change the way a reader, customer, consumer, subscriber, or user "thinks." You are successful when you've moved their thinking from the old way to the *new and different way* you are educating them about. But what is "thinking"?

According to Roger Martin, often referred to as the world's number one management thinker, "thinking" is when you look at the world through an existing model. It's how you use learnings from the past to make sense of the present. For example, when another driver cuts you off on the highway, you instantly apply your past experiences to the present and swerve to avoid an accident.

Your reflex saves your life.

But here's the rub: Almost all thinking is what Roger calls "reflexive."

- **"Reflexive" thinking:** having an unconscious "reflex" in response to ideas or opinions

- **"Reflective" thinking:** taking a moment to consciously reflect on how the past may have created a preexisting mental model keeping you from considering a new and different future

For example, imagine someone says, "If you're not for the first amendment, then you're anti-American."

The recipient of this opinion experiences a reflex, as if a doctor slammed a tiny pink hammer against their kneecap and their leg jolts upward. They immediately respond with, "I'm not anti-American! You're anti-American for even thinking that about me!" This exchange is akin to the mental retweeting of information these people agree with or disagree with—and it lacks meaningful *reflection*.

Some of the smartest people stopped reflective thinking a long time ago. We would even go so far as to say that being declared a smart person is almost certain to make you stupid. Because when you get called "smart," you become entrenched in your comfortable past. When you're smart, you know things—and most people who know things are called "experts." Which means they *already* know. And when you already know, by definition, you are using old mental scaffolding to consider new and different futures.

This makes you stupid.

But thinking about "the past" is deeply rooted in the DNA of many entrepreneurs, investors, executives, academics, and strategists. The vast majority of content about strategic thinking comes from academia and strategy consulting firms. When you hire management consulting firms, what you're mostly buying is a detailed analysis of what worked *yesterday*. This is exactly what technology analyst firms like Gartner do—they explain the past.

Academia takes it one step further. The pinnacle of being an economics or business school professor is winning the Nobel Prize. But the Nobel Prize in economics is typically awarded for work completed *decades ago*, based on analyses of data even before that!

- Harvard Business School students read approximately five hundred case studies about the past during their two years of study.

- Most management consulting firms give a detailed analysis of what worked *yesterday*. They explain the past.

- Academics can't publish without extensive research about the past. Any new information has to be rigorously peer-reviewed by other professors who are experts in the past.

These are not accurate or effective definitions of truly strategic thinking.

The core issue is that 100 percent of what we've been taught is based on the past and doesn't reflect a future where many things might change. Every generation looks and laughs at prior generations and wonders, "How did those prior generations believe that? Look at what we didn't know!"

Well, why do we assume future generations won't look at us the same way?

Don't strive to become an expert, ever! Expertise is the enemy of fresh thinking.

To change the world, and define and dominate a category, you have to reject the premise. You can't rely on mental scaffolding built in *the past*. You can't just blindly accept the world the way it is. You have to reject the way *it is* to create the way *it will be*.

Because every legendary company was a dumb idea, until it wasn't.

Here's How Category Designers Think

Actual "thinking" is not reflexive. It's reflective.

You are presented with information. You become conscious of which model you are using to evaluate the information, the "lens" you are looking through. And then *before* you react, respond, or give in to your reflexive nature, you pause and first consider which mental model you're using to examine the information being presented. You train yourself to be curious, to ask why, to suspend your past opinions, beliefs, and mental models, and to open the aperture of your mind and consider something different.

That's "thinking."

This is very different from what most people do, which is play a game of "I'm right, you're wrong" ping-pong. You talk, I talk; you talk, I talk. But no one is listening or thinking. They're just waiting to talk.

With the above in mind, "strategic thinking"—maybe one of the most overused yet misunderstood phrases in all of academia and business—is not what most people think it is.

For example, Pirate Christopher remembers a conversation with a young, early-stage entrepreneur. She explained she had "good news" and "bad news." The good news was that the data confirmed they had reached a place where 50 percent of the solution was working for the problem they had promised to solve. The "bad news" was that 50 percent was not working.

Pirate Christopher explained that this was all good news.

At first, this shocked the young entrepreneur. But Pirate Christopher said, "We're in creation-and-discovery mode. We just confirmed the core idea for the business and the category is right, and we validated 50 percent of our business model. That's a legendary outcome."

If you look at the results through a "we have to get everything right at the very start lens," then yes, this news was part "bad." But when you look at the same data through the lens of thirty-seven years of category design and entrepreneurial experience, it's all great news. Because only with an experience lens can you evaluate the progress of something. The first-timer has no point of reference.

You train yourself to be curious, to ask why, to suspend

your past opinions, beliefs, and mental models, and to open the aperture of your mind and consider something different.

That's "thinking."

Strategic thinking, in its purest form, is the process of considering "what could be true."

Strategy is the art of the possible.

- What new mental model would have to be invented for this to work?
- What if people moved *from* the way it is, *to* a new, different way?
- What if a new outcome (an outcome we haven't considered before) was possible?

You have to stand in the future to create a different future. Our friend, Mike Maples Jr., calls this "backcasting."

Legendary builders must stand in the future and pull the present from the current reality to the future of their design. So an important additional job of the builder is to persuade early like-minded people to join a new movement.

But how do you give people context that excites them enough to meet you in the future and join a new movement? (This is a very powerful question to reflect upon.) You give them a new point of view they can grab onto and repeat to their friends, who will tell their friends, and so on, and so on.

Here are a few powerful examples:

- "Gay Rights"
- "Equal Pay for Equal Work"
- "Undocumented Immigrants"

The most effective POVs aim conventional thinking and conversation in a wildly different direction. Oftentimes, it's hard for the masses to understand or accept what this new POV might mean for the world. (Sun Microsystems was an early pioneer in the tech industry that contributed an incredible amount of knowledge and had one of the greatest category designing taglines in history: "The network is the computer." It forced thinking and caused a conversation.)

An easy exercise to *start* thinking is understanding whether you are forecasting or backcasting.

Take a moment to think about which direction you are facing:

- **Forecasting:** standing in the past, looking forward, thinking about the future
- **Backcasting:** standing in a different future and living "as if" that different future already exists today

This might seem like an inconsequential nuance, but it is the starting point that defines the entire trajectory of your company and/or creative act.

If you start with the way the world "is," then try to make the way it "is" different, you are making an unconscious decision to improve **within the context of a game someone else invented**. You are competing. But if you start with the way it "could be," if you assume the possible and stand in the future, you give yourself the opportunity to write new rules for the game you are inventing. You are creating.

You are unencumbered by the past and present.

Now, backcasting is a good way to get your mind in a different place. But in order to act on those fresh, future-oriented ideas swirling around in your mind, you have to understand the difference between Obvious and Non-Obvious content.

- **Obvious Content**: The art of speaking to what people already think and believe, catering to the reader's reflexive nature
- **Non-Obvious Content**: The art of educating people on what they haven't thought about or decided they believe yet, requesting their reflective nature

It's crucial to understand which of these two states you are creating for, whether you are creating a new category, a new company, or a new piece of content. You have to know where you are "meeting the consumer" long before you take action.

If you try feeding Non-Obvious content that requires reflection and challenging one's own mental models to someone in an Obvious (reflexive) state, you will fail to get their attention and/or they'll likely become frustrated at your inability to cater to their preconceived notions. And conversely, if you try feeding Obvious content to someone starving for Non-Obvious insights, you will either burden

them with boredom or they will become frustrated with—
and maybe even insulted by—you wasting their time.
("This is so obvious! Make me think!")

- **Reflexive** thinkers want Obvious content.
- **Reflective** thinkers want Non-Obvious content.

Becoming a reflective thinker who knows who you are creating for and what their expectations are (and why) is half
the battle to becoming a legendary category designer.

Reflective Thinking That Rejects the Premise Lets You Create a Different Future

No legendary entrepreneur, business leader, or creator
started their journey by accepting the premise.

- Why did hotels sue Airbnb, calling them "illegal
  hotels"? *Because Airbnb's POV changed the premise.*
- How did Picasso become one of the most well-
  known and highly valued artists of all time? *Because
  he "quit" the game of Impressionism and "created"
  a new game called Cubism.*
- What made Cirque du Soleil a billion-dollar business
  with more than four thousand employees perform-
  ing shows in over forty countries? *Co-founders Guy
  Laliberté and Gilles Ste-Croix were on a mission to
  create performative, acrobatic, animal-free theater,
  NOT start a better circus.*

The vast majority of people take whatever is placed in front
of them and say, "I accept the premise." (They actually
don't even do that. They unconsciously accept the way it is,

with no consideration for the way it could be.)

They start with the way it is and aim to make the way it is "better." *Something exists. Then this new thing came along. And we're going to apply the new thing to the old thing and call the old thing new.* There is very little questioning about whether they are having the right conversation (context) to begin with. As a result, a company's (or creator's) POV is unconsciously established, and every product, document, and decision that unfolds from there follows that POV. And this results in a lifetime of comparison and competition.

If history has taught us anything, it's that exponential outcomes are produced by strategic, future-oriented thinkers.

These thinkers rejected the way *it was* in order to create the way *it would be.*

For example, the idea of Airbnb made no sense when evaluated through old mental models. As a result, nearly every venture capitalist said, "No way. You can't rent out your extra bedroom. That's insane. Probably illegal. What if someone gets killed in their sleep or raped? And you really think people will want to share a toilet with someone they've never met before?"

Only a very small handful of investors (including the world-class firm Sequoia Capital) had the courage and mental awareness to ask a different question—a "thinking" question:

"What would need to be true for this idea to work?"

They realized that the idea of Airbnb didn't make sense when evaluated through previously established mental models, but it *did* make sense through the lens of a new model. In fact, it was likely a decade away from being completely acceptable—and thus, "worth the risk" (which helped Sequoia turn roughly $280 million invested over multiple rounds into more than $12 billion). Every legendary business is a dumb idea—until it isn't.

Why is this important for category designers to understand?

Rejecting the premise helps you recognize future opportunities.

Ford and Tesla are the only two American car companies at scale that have not gone bankrupt. The car category is a highly capital-intensive one with razor-thin margins. But Ford's Model T (sold from 1908 to 1927) was the first ever car that mainstream Americans could afford to buy. As Ford and other internal combustion cars grew, the company created massive abundance for customers, employees, and shareholders. A new category was born.

The success of the Model T paved the way for the success of the Model S, X, 3, and Y from Tesla. This may seem surprising. Internal combustion engine (ICE) cars rely on fossil fuels, which are nonrenewable and limited in supply. This is the exact opposite of Tesla's electric vehicles and its mission to accelerate the world's transition to sustainable energy.

Let's reject the premise for a moment to see the opportunity here.

The industrial revolution of the eighteenth and nineteenth centuries provided the technological advancements (ICE technology) and materials Ford needed to mass produce the Model T. This made cars practical and affordable. At the time, people didn't fully understand the negative environmental impact of ICE cars and fossil fuels. In fact, many people saw the Model T as a symbol of progress and freedom.

Today, the environmental impact of cars is a major concern.

By rejecting the premise and imagining the future, we can see that yesterday's solution (ICE cars) is today's problem (air pollution), which becomes tomorrow's solution (electric vehicles).

Here are a few more examples:

- Yesterday, processed foods saved lives from contamination and bacteria. Today, processed foods are a major factor in obesity, which can result in chronic health issues.

- Yesterday, college and higher education allowed Americans to realize the American Dream. Today, college is responsible for $1.8 trillion dollars of student loan debt—and excessive debt is the reason consumers are held back from buying a house or starting a family.

- Yesterday, smartphones allowed people to hold the internet in their hands. Today, our addiction to smartphones allowed Apple (the same company that fueled the addiction) to sell smartwatches, which make it easier to detach from our smartphones.

The takeaway: You have opportunities to engage in reflective thinking and reject the premise *everywhere*, but you must get the timing right to create a category-defining solution.

Exercise: Start Rejecting the Premise

To engage in reflective thinking, we encourage you to ask a series of thoughtful questions:

1. Steelmanning an argument is the process of presenting the strongest version of the opposite side of your original argument. It's a way of being intellectually honest and open-minded about a point of view you have. In the last month, how often did you steelman an opposing argument?

2. Think about the past week. How many hours did you spend reflective thinking?

3. Many of us hold several beliefs about business as gospel. For example: "Be number one or number two in your industry," "Best practices and benchmarking are the truth," or "First mover advantage." Make a list of your top five core business beliefs.

   ➤ _____

   ➤ _____

   ➤ _____

   ➤ _____

   ➤ _____

Are you sure these beliefs are still true in the age of category design?

- When was the last time you "rejected the premise"

of a major bit of conventional wisdom in your business? Did it result in a negative or positive outcome?

- Think about a current Non-Obvious idea you have but haven't shared widely or acted on. What is it? Why haven't you shared it or acted on it? How much abundance could you unlock if you shared or acted on it?

Now that you are thinking reflectively, ask yourself the following questions to figure out the new and different solutions you want to create in the world.

4. What are the most prevalent solutions considered "universally good" in your category today? Write down the top five below:

➤ _____

_____

➤ _____

_____

➤ _____

_____

➤ _____

_____

➤ _____

_____

5. Take each of those solutions to the extreme by imagining what would happen if a consumer indulges too much in the solution. For example, what would happen if someone indulged in too much fast food? Too many online courses? Too many medications? Write down what might happen for each solution and if it is a net positive or negative outcome.

➤ _____

_____

➤ _____

_____

➤ _____

_____

➤ _____

_____

➤ _____

_____

6. You now have five problems to choose from. Whittle it down to the three options that excite you the most. Your reasoning could be because you think the problem will happen sooner, you have something unique to offer that can help, or you think it will be the biggest opportunity. For example, fast fashion has become a problem in recent years. So companies have begun creating "tomorrow's solution" with responsible manufacturing practices, sustainable materials use, and business models that promote a circular economy.

➤ _____

_____

➤ _____

_____

➤ _____

_____

7. For each option, develop a point of view that describes what you would do to create "tomorrow's solution" for "today's problem." Write about the breakthrough offer, the breakthrough business

model, and any breakthrough data you can provide. For example, Patagonia, a well-known outdoor clothing company, created a program called Worn Wear that encourages customers to repair and reuse their clothing rather than buying new items.

➤ _____

_____

➤ _____

_____

➤ _____

_____

8. Sometimes, the future is already here. Specific "Super-Geo" locations can show where the local market is far ahead of the rest of the world. For example, circular fashion is gaining momentum in the Netherlands, Scandinavia, and San Francisco. A Super-Geo can be a physical location (a city or zip code), digital area (a specific digital community), or vocational (a specific profession).

Pick one of the three POVs from above, and write down the top five Super-Geos where you think tomorrow's solution would be welcome today.

➤ _____

_____

➤ _____

_____

➤ _____

_____

➤ _____

_____

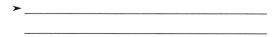

The rest of this book will teach you the strategies and frameworks you need to act on your solutions.

Companies, entrepreneurs, and investors who reject the premise, proactively facilitate unconstrained creative discussions about the future, and are *willing to strategize and build what doesn't exist yet* are the ones who escape the rat race of competition and enter the promised land of creation. Once you've glimpsed the future, you then need to plant your flag and tell people how it will be different. This is just the beginning of designing a new category, and there is much more to it than building a great product, company, or brand.

We'll explain why this has an exponential economic benefit in the next chapter.

The Category Queen of a Given Market Captures 76 Percent of the Economics

Companies that create new categories, or successfully redesign existing categories, create exponentially more value for both shareholders and the entire market.

Category designers introduce the world to new ways of living, working, and playing.

They are people and companies who move the world *from* the way it is, *to* the way they think it should be. And they do this by solving a problem people didn't know they had or by reimagining a known problem, then creating the potential for a radically different solution. Most of all, they create (and subsequently capture) the exponential new value generated by an ecosystem of employees, customers, partners, investors, and communities.

To make sure our category design Kool-Aid tastes as good as we think it does, we conducted a set of studies to wrap our brains around the difference between category creators and other fast-growing, successful businesses. In 2021, we analyzed the Fortune 100 fast-growing companies list from 2009 to 2018. We pulled data from their 10Ks, annual reports, investor presentations, and investor relations websites. And what we found wowed us.

Only 19 percent of the fast-growing companies were category creators.

Stunningly, the category creators captured the vast majority of the growth: 51 percent of the prior three years cumulative revenue growth and 80 percent of the prior three years market capitalization.

That's not just *differentiation*.

That's *radical differentiation*.

Category-Designing Companies Create Exponentially More Value

Companies that create new categories, or successfully redesign existing categories, create exponentially more value for both shareholders and the entire market. Ultimately, category designers change the world. Now, if there's data that supports our thesis that category design is the fastest, most effective way to grow, then why do so many companies insist on competing?

Fortune 500 companies have the hardest time understanding category design as a growth strategy.

They are conservative for a reason.

They have stuff to conserve. That stuff is everything from existing market share to quarterly company profits to investor relationships to balance sheet optics. In most large companies, and in many existing smaller companies, executives get paid to "Not f*ck things up."

These incumbent companies are often themselves aging Category Kings. They were once the rebel-headed upstart pioneering new territory in the business landscape, but they are now stuck defending the slow-moving, slow-growing category with which they've become synonymous. So much so, that many feel no urgency to change despite incrementally growing profits year over year.

The unfortunate reality is that the fear of losing what ground they have today is greater than the exponential value that could be generated by embracing category innovation tomorrow. These companies live out their days bound like hostages to the tyranny of quarterly expectations, trying to convince themselves, their employees, and their shareholders there is still "a bit more juice left in the squeeze."

Successful companies of the past rarely stay alive long enough to create the future.

They stop creating and start protecting.

Here is a good example. In the '80s and '90s, business professionals admired General Electric (GE) and its CEO, Jack Welch, above all companies and executives. Welch had a specific view on corporate strategy. You should be number one or number two in your industry, or you should exit the business. That was good advice before the internet came along. But it is terrible advice on the advent of artificial intelligence and machine learning.

The digital transformation age began in the early 2000s, and it is now influencing one of the most profound shifts happening in the world.

For the first time in history, there are two different types of people on earth.

- **The first are Native Analogs.** These are Baby Boomers and Gen Xers, born anywhere from the 1940s all the way up to the early '80s. Today, they range between the ages of 4 to 77, and make up approximately 136.8 million Americans.

- **The second are Native Digitals.** These are Millennials and Gen Zers, born between the early 1980s to as recently as the 2010s. In 2023, they range between the ages of 40 on the high end today, down to as young as 11 years old and make up approximately 140.1 million Americans.

The difference?

Native Analogs grew up in a time where technology was an addition or, better yet, a distraction from their real lives.

Native digitals grew up in a time where their real lives were a distraction from their digital lives.

This is a major shift and few people are talking about it. Even more stunning, some of the largest native digital brands on the planet are run by native analogs who don't get it either. But it will impact every category on earth, if it has not already. The result of this macro trend is that if you are 40 years old or younger, you will progressively spend more time, energy, and money enhancing yourself in your digital life than you will in your analog life.

You can see this shift from valuing "stuff" to valuing digital products, experiences, and personal transformation everywhere:

- 74% of Americans now value experiences more than physical products, the majority of whom are Millennials

- Cryptocurrencies and non-fungible tokens (NFTs) are becoming a primary store of value

- Every client/server enterprise tech company is making the transition to the cloud

In the physical world, customers value physical products. In the digital world, customers value digital products. In a world where digital goods are seen as more valuable (or equally as valuable) as physical goods, we can see the future reflect that transfer of value. Physical goods are giving way to digital services, products, experiences, and other "non-stuff" sectors. That mean categories that make "stuff" need to innovate digital products and services to go along with their physical products.

The takeaway here is that the economics of digital goods are much greater than physical goods.

That's because digital businesses have increasing returns business models.

In the analog world, costs are pegged to sales. If Starbucks wants to grow, it needs to build physical stores. On the other hand, the cost for eBay to serve 10 customers or 10,000 customers is incremental. That's what makes digital businesses *increasing-returns businesses.*

In the new Native Digital world, only the number one company wins.

The way it wins is by designing and dominating a new and different category. How? By learning how to see the world through a category lens. That means understanding and applying the principles of category design and category creation.

Category design research shows the Category King or Queen of a given market captures 76 percent of the economics.

But most business leaders spend their entire careers

competing for the remaining 24 percent of the value opportunity of a given category. This fascinated Pirate Eddie, so he analyzed a ton of Nielsen data to dig deeper. And he found that if a category is growing, one percent of the brands capture 80 percent of category growth.

There can only be one winner.

That said, winning is more nuanced in today's world.

Being number one in a digital category is far superior to being number one in an analog category. This is why Airbnb trades at 8x revenue versus Marriott which trades at 2.5x revenue. If you are number one in an analog category, you can pivot to the digital version of your category. If you are number one in a digital category, congrats! You recognized the macro trends hiding in plain sight, capitalized on them, and are riding a tailwind into the future. A category design rule of thumb is that new categories beget new categories, so keep your eyes on the horizon for the next opportunity.

For anyone who is number two in a category, be prepared to cap your upside at 24 percent of the category market cap. But if you're a piratey type of entrepreneur or executive who refuses to be capped at 24 percent, we have some good news for you. There are several category design strategies at your disposal to change your company's lot in life.

There are three strategies you can use to capture the majority of a category's economic value: mergers and acquisitions, spinning out the buried treasures within your company, and using category design.

Let's break down each one:

Use Mergers and Acquisitions

Mergers and acquisitions (M&A) transactions are a great way to leapfrog from number two in an analog category to number one in a digital category. And while you have to use bankers and consultants to execute the M&A, you should be prescriptive about what kind of M&A you want to execute. Because in category design, there is a right and wrong way to go about it.

If you want to grow your revenues and category dominance, you can choose between two acquisition approaches:

- **Acceleration:** Buy the leader in an emerging or tangentially relevant category (or the missing ingredient needed to redesign your current category) to accelerate your position in the future

- **Consolidation:** Buy a competitor in a slow-growth, shrinking category to bulk-up your position and achieve economies of scale

Wall Street loves consolidation deals because they are familiar and investors know what to expect. Category designers avoid them at all costs. (For fun, we like to take a gulp of rum every time the word "synergy" appears in a publicly-traded company's M&A press release.)

Acceleration deals can work if you are clear on the desired outcome. It's not to be the winner and earn the majority of market share. It's not to be the best company with the best product.

It's to be different.

Here is a bit more detail on what that looks like, based on an analysis we did of the category economics of the Fortune 100 Fastest-Growing Companies list:

- **Be the Winner:** These companies are market share maniacs with no goal other than to beat their competitors and be the number one market share leader. They believe things like "brand equity" will be the reason customers pick their products off the shelf.

- **Be the Best:** These companies want to be seen in the market as having the best product, service, or technology. They are innovation and R&D focused but exclusively through the lens of having the best tech or product for the sake of being able to win comparison debates against existing competitors.

- **Be Different:** These companies end up writing or rewriting the rules of the game by creating a new category or redesigning an existing category. They drive the Be the Winner and Be the Best companies out of business or out of relevance by creating a different future.

This topic deserves several chapters, which we don't have the space for here. If you want to learn more, you can pick up our mini-book *Radical M&A Strategy: The Difference Between Accelerating and Consolidating A Category.*

Mergers and acquisitions are not the only way to create more value within your company.

Spin Out Your Hidden Gem

Your analog company may be number two in its category, but you might be sitting on a hidden gem that could make you number one in a digital company. For example, eBay did this when it spun out Paypal in 2015. At the time, PayPal had $9.2 billion in revenue. In 2022, PayPal had $27.5 billion in revenue with companies like Venmo, Hyperwallet, and Braintree in its portfolio.

How do you know if you are sitting on a hidden gem?

You run a category size of prize (aka, category potential) analysis.

This is important because savvy growth investors do not buy just your company's performance in an existing category. They buy your potential in an exciting, emerging, and fast-growing new category that is creating a different future. As a category designer and company leader, it is your job to sell them on that potential if you are trying to spin out an asset.

This drives growth in four ways:

1. It adds credence to your words, story, and POV of your new category.

2. It adds clarity to your number one priority, so you avoid shiny new toys and strategically build the mission-critical beachhead you need to dominate the entire category.

3. It adds conviction to your actions, so you go big when building the category.

4. It accelerates all outcomes, which increases your credibility, conviction, and clarity.

Together, these factors help drive the valuation of your category and company.

But a legacy size of prize analysis is not comprehensive enough to reveal a category's true potential. Oftentimes, "experts" fail to estimate the future market cap value of radically different categories and the companies that dominate them. That's because category potential is a hard concept for reflexive thinking number-crunchers to wrap their minds around. So, they get the estimates wrong. They either underestimate the opportunity, like how Kodak invented the digital camera but failed to capitalize on its mass-market potential. Or they overestimate the opportunity, like how Quibi raised $1.8 billion in funding for its mobile video-streaming platform but shipwrecked just six months after launch.

Getting market cap estimates directionally right is the key to consistently driving revenue, attracting investor interest, and accelerating your category's (and company's) growth.

The category size of prize process has four main steps:

- **Step 1**: Be crystal clear on the context.
- **Step 2**: Triage, tag, and triangulate existing data.
- **Step 3**: Create new, credible data where it is most needed.
- **Step 4**: Put the puzzle together, make a decision, and tell a story.

Most people skip steps one and four, so they do the size of prize analysis in a vacuum. This approach treats it as a purely technical and analytical exercise, which allows the work to be critiqued in a purely technical and analytical way. Oftentimes, the result is a painful experience where executives and analysts throw equation eggs and technical tomatoes at you. But you can avoid this by understanding the context and telling a story to explain your results.

That said, let's walk through each step.

Step 1: Be Crystal Clear On The Context

A size of prize analysis isn't GAAP accounting, so there is no "right way" to do it.

Instead, context is king. That's because the value of a size of prize analysis is in the eye of the beholder. Doing a back-of-the-envelope analysis can work in a situation where speed and directional guidance are all you need. But if you're doing due diligence and there is a data room involved, having detailed data sets and a clear backup to every spreadsheet matters.

To figure out the context and the depth of your analysis, answer these three questions:

1. Who is the audience for the analysis?
2. What decisions will they make based on it?
3. Given the audience and decisions, how deep must it go?
   - Solo-worthy: It is good enough for me and my own thoughts.
   - Social media-worthy: It is robust enough to risk my neck on a POV and defend it.
   - S-1-worthy: It is credible and compelling enough to use for an initial public offering (IPO).

If you skip this step, the definition of success (aka, the prize) becomes infinite and the analysis morphs into a Nostradamus exercise. The only way to succeed at that point is to get the precise number and dates right. But if you answer these questions before running the analysis, you'll understand what you need to deliver massive value to your audience. Clear answers give you far more grace around your actual numbers and help you and your audience make important decisions.

Step 2: Triage, Tag, And Triangulate Existing Data

Once you know the context, you're ready to collect and categorize two types of data.

The first type is available data about the past and present. Think of this as performance data. This could be early sales data from a startup or innovation or data from the ultra-high end or ultra-low end of an existing category. All of this is valuable and real, so it must be included—but be wary of putting too many eggs in this basket.

(Benchmarking the past is fine for incremental strategies and line extensions, but it falls flat when you're creating an entirely new category.)

You can categorize this data into a few buckets:

- Accounting data that requires third-party scrutiny (sales, profits, etc.)
- Benchmarking data that requires a credible source (like Nielsen market shares)
- Cross-functional performance data (turnover for HR,

ROIC for finance, etc.)

The second type is data about the future. Think of this as "potential data." This could be extrapolated forecasts based on the past, data from surveys, or data from "what if" analyses. Much of this information will be inaccurate in the actual numbers, but it can be quite accurate in the fundamental trendline and slope of the data.

You can use the following buckets to group this data:

- Near-term demand that is easily quantifiable (orders received, pipeline, etc.)
- Trend data from a credible source (predictions from McKinsey, Gartner, etc.)
- Cross-functional potential data (recruiting demand, innovation pipeline, etc.)

Every size of prize analysis should be a triangulation of performance data about the past/present and potential data about the future.

Any analysis that is too one-sided will miss the mark.

Most importantly, you don't want to pit performance data against potential data. Instead, you want to see where there is overlap and disagreement in the data. You can then isolate the specific areas of disagreement and dig deeper into the data quality by asking:

- What are the weaknesses of each data set?
- What are the fatal flaws and Achilles' heel assumptions?

- What if I had new data to help me break the tie?

Your goal here is to identify data gaps, not to come to a conclusion right away. Triangulate the data to see where the current data is robust, where it is strong, and where it is lacking. You can then start to form your hypothesis, which will help you with the next step.

Step 3: Create New, Credible Data Where It Is Most Needed

Many people overlook this step.

That's because new data is typically created in big, multi-year studies at academic institutions, think tanks, or big consulting firms looking to publish thought leadership. Creating new data for a one-off size of prize analysis may not be your first instinct. (But you're reading this book, so we know you're capable of thinking different!)

When carefully crafted, new data will increase the value of your size of prize analysis.

You can create three types of new data:

1. **Opinion Fact-Base Data.** To get this information, you aggregate opinions from customers, investors, or other "key opinion leaders" to get their perspective on the future. You can do these through customer surveys or one-on-one interviews.

   - Pros: Done correctly, this data can be very powerful. This is especially true if you do it on a representative sample that can be calibrated and projected nationally or globally and ask the right questions in the right way.

- Cons: Done incorrectly, this data can be quite misleading and cause you to make unhelpful decisions. Coca-Cola's extinct "New Coke" product is a case in point. When launching a new flavor formula, the company asked consumers the wrong question, "Do you prefer the taste of New Coke or Classic Coke?" instead of asking the right question, "Do you want to replace Classic Coke with New Coke?" Consumers answered "yes" to the first question and a resounding "no" to the second.

2. **Outcomes Fact-Base Data.** This type of data gathers outcomes, which you can use to make inferences about the future. To create it, you can run a small pilot or adopt a "test-and-learn" approach. This is typically done through A/B testing with a control group or, even better, with your Super-Geos—local markets with higher demand per capita. (You will learn more about Super-Geos in a later chapter.)

   - Pros: Well-executed outcomes data will always be more valuable than well-executed opinion data because consumers' actions speak louder than their words. When creating this data, Super-Geos may already be telling you about the future, without you having to test it (think: California for EVs or the Pacific Northwest for Craft Beer).

   - Cons: It can be easy to make errors with the test-and-learn approach and pilots, which require a lot of practice to do well and interpret properly.

3. **Super-Geos Fact-Base Data.** This is the ultimate form of new data to create because it combines the best of the opinion fact-base and outcomes fact-base data.

- Pros: Super-Geos have real outcomes (like higher spending per capita) and make for ideal places to run credible tests and pilots. But Super-Geos are "super" because there is a high density of Superconsumers within them. You can aggregate opinion data within the Super-Geo to explain the "why" as well as the "what."

- Cons: It takes a bit more thinking about thinking to create this data. But we cover how to find your Super-Geos in the final chapter of this book.

The amount and rigor of new data you need to create are directly connected to the "how deep must the analysis go" question you asked earlier. If this is a solo-worthy size of prize, then one to two in-depth conversations with a consumer might be all you need. If you are going to post a thoughtful piece about your category's potential, you will want to create more outcome data to strengthen your POV. If you need new data for an S-1, you will want to go to the Super-Geo fact-base level.

Start with your end goal, and then decide what data to create.

Step 4: Put the Pieces Together, Make a Decision, and Tell a Story

Many people think the size of prize analysis is all numbers and math. That is a huge part of it, but this analysis only has real value if you make decisions based on what you find. It is not meant to be a nitpicky discussion of why you did not round that decimal here or there.

The size of prize is designed to help you move forward on a go/no-go decision.

Should you invest or not? Should you push that innovation forward or not? Should you work at that company or not?

The best way to answer those questions is to construct a story.

You don't need the best discount cash flow analysis to tell a story about your legendary outcome. Instead, your job is to assemble the size of prize puzzle as best as you can with your triaged, tagged, and triangulated data juxtaposed next to your created data. And then, let the data sit for a bit to see what story it tells.

Look at it close up, and then take a big step back. What catches your eye?

You will notice patterns, weird delightful surprises, and information that meet your expectations. Next, you want to take all that data and revisit the audience and decision part of the process from step one. Frame the data in the context of your audience and the decisions to be made. Then, make your decision.

For detailed examples, you can dive deeper into our Category Pirates mini-book *Sizing The Category Prize*.

The bottom line is the conventional strategies of competing for market share or building the best product or brand are largely irrelevant if you end up as number two or number one in an analog category. The most important strategy for earning the majority of a category's economics is being number one in a primarily digital category that is radically different from the conventional category.

If that sounds enticing to you, keep reading and applying the strategies in this book.

Use Category Design to Become the Category King

This is our favorite way of doing it. Category design helps companies win in a native digital world by creating radically different ideas, pairing those ideas with language that sticks, and scaling them through digital word-of-mouth marketing. The laws within this book are the foundational frameworks and strategies you need to make your category a reality.

The next chapter will help set you up for success.

Your Category Is the Single Point of Failure (the Magic Triangle)

If you don't have clarity on your category, no amount of product tweaking or business-model banging will make a difference.

Many companies have succeeded with a shoddy product. Many have succeeded with a lousy business or brand. But no company has ever succeeded without a successful category. No category, no market. No market, no company.

Your category is your single point of failure.

For example, certain industries create "marketing boards" that promote and protect the category on behalf of all the players in the space. This is the origin story behind the legendary "Got Milk?" campaign. It didn't come from a milk farm brand—it came from the California Milk Processor Board. Why do milk producers pay to promote their category? Because your category is your single point of failure. It's tough to grow 30 percent in a category that's shrinking by 10 percent.

That's why one of the first things you hear public market investors say when talking about why they invested in a new company is "I like the space."

You can see this happening in the tech industry, especially in B2B tech. In a 2023 study title "Tech Is Cooling Off. B2B SaaS Is Not", the Boston Consulting Group found that the global B2B SaaS industry is growing at an average 17 percent per year. But IBM, a legacy computing company, grew by 3.6 percent in 2023. Given that IBM isn't designing new categories, it's not creating net-new demand. So, its growth is pegged to the growth of the B2B SaaS category. If the category starts shrinking, IBM will also shrink.

The Category Makes the Company

We would like to introduce you to a new lens for interpreting the business world called "The Magic Triangle."

This lens can dramatically improve your odds of becoming a category leader, what we call a Category King or Queen. Because once you see the world through The Magic Triangle, you'll never see things the same way again.

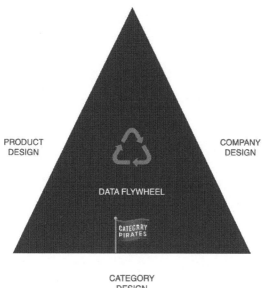

The Magic Triangle has three sides: product design, company design, and category design.

- **Product design:** The purposeful building of a product and experience that solves the problem the category needs solved. The goal here is "product/category fit."

- **Company design:** The purposeful creation of a business model and an organization with a culture and point of view that fits with the new category. The goal here is to engineer the right business model and missionary team for the problem you are looking to solve.

- **Category design:** The mindful creation and development of a new market category, designed so the category will pull in customers who will then make the company its king. This is about teaching the world to abandon the old and embrace the new.

All three sides work together and balance each other to exert great force on a company's success and value.

When entrepreneurs successfully prosecute this Magic Triangle, they change the world.

The big question is "How?" Let's look at three examples from Category Kings DoorDash, Tesla, and Lomi.

DoorDash started as a local delivery service in Palo Alto, California.

Today, DoorDash is an international Category King that operates in more than seven thousand cities across the United States, Canada, Australia, and Japan. Here's how it synchronized all three sides of the Magic Triangle to dominate food delivery.

Product design: In 2012, four Stanford students (Tony Xu, Stanley Tang, Andy Fang, and Evan Moore) went door-to-door interviewing local business owners. In a small macaroon shop, they realized one of the owner's core issues—deliveries. She didn't have any drivers to fulfill orders, so she delivered everything herself. The students heard the same thing over and over: deliveries are painful.

In a detailed 2020 Twitter thread that explained DoorDash's growth, co-founder Evan Moore told the story: "We found that restaurants had a more acute pain point. Most didn't deliver, and the few that did *hated* doing it. It made no sense for a restaurant to have its own delivery people when they could have five orders one day, twenty the next—a pooled resource would obviously be better."

Company design: After setting up a delivery service, the four students started delivering food from local restaurants to other students on campus. They quickly had a breakthrough. Most restaurants in the Palo Alto area didn't deliver, even though there was customer demand for it. They realized their order fulfillment and delivery business model was viable and possible.

So, they began convincing restaurants to try the service.

"That restaurant delivery was such a large opportunity was counterintuitive even to us. There were many (crummy) local services around. But at this point, the latent demand for restaurant delivery was slapping us in the face," Moore said in the same Twitter thread.

Category design: Naturally, DoorDash faced competition from local delivery services. But Moore shared the company's key to becoming a Category King. "We were able to be far more efficient than our competitors even before our series A, just from smartly solving for an on-demand model with three sides."

The three sides: delighting customers, merchants, and drivers.

Moore also commented on the competition, "We ignored them. We stayed focused on delighting customers, merchants, and drivers. That company is long dead." Today, DoorDash commands over 60 percent of the U.S. food-delivery market share. Its closest competitors? Uber Eats at 31 percent and Grubhub at 9 percent.

Now, let's look at how Tesla used the Magic Triangle.

Since 2003, Elon Musk has been announcing to the world, "We believe internal combustion engines are polluting the planet and contributing to global warming, and we are going to work toward solving this problem by inventing electric vehicles at scale."

That's why Tesla is not just a car manufacturer—it's a sustainable energy manufacturer.

Product design: Tesla simply began by building zero-emission vehicles. And its mission, *accelerating the world's transition to sustainable energy,* is apparent in every product it designs.

- **Zero-emission electric vehicle:** replacing petroleum-based fuels (90 percent of transportation energy in the U.S.) with clean energy
- **Solar panels:** replacing electricity produced by fossil fuels (60 percent of electric energy in the U.S.) with clean energy
- **Batteries that store clean energy:** reducing residential greenhouse gas emissions (emissions from businesses and homes are primarily from fossil fuels)

Tesla's products not only fit the company's mission, but they also fit a specific sustainable energy need.

Company design: Category designers have no secrets when it comes to their visions for the world, which is why Elon Musk open-sourced Tesla's patents for any company to use. The following is an excerpt from the company's 2014 announcement that shared the news:

> *Tesla Motors was created to accelerate the advent of sustainable transport. If we clear a path to the creation of compelling electric vehicles but then lay intellectual property landmines behind us to inhibit others, we are acting in a manner contrary to that goal. Tesla will not initiate patent lawsuits against anyone who, in good faith, wants to use our technology.*

Elon Musk understands that Tesla alone cannot achieve the mission of building electric cars fast enough to address the carbon crisis. So, he made Tesla's intellectual property accessible. *The more, the merrier.* On top of that, he also refused to partner with car dealerships so Tesla can sell its vehicles at fixed, easy-to-understand prices.

Category design: Tesla doesn't promote the "Tesla" brand. They promote "electric vehicles" and, more broadly, the "sustainable energy" category. Like all category designers and Category Kings, Elon Musk and Tesla do not fit into old boxes. They are new. They are different. They cannot be compared to what came before.

Once you go Tesla, you don't go back. That's because no other car brand is a credible substitute for a Tesla. And as of writing, Tesla is the dominant electric vehicle company in the U.S. with about 63 percent market share.

Lomi co-founders shared a passion for making a difference on Mother Earth.

Lomi, a smart home composter, was the most successful crowdfunded environmental product of 2021. The company's co-founders, Jeremy Lang, Matt Bertulli, and Brad Pedersen, are on a mission to make at-home food waste a thing of the past. So they leveraged all three sides of the Magic Triangle to design a new category.

Product design: Lomi's founders had a vision for an elegant kitchen device that would get rid of disgusting food waste while also turning an environmentally damaging source of carbon into highly nutrient-dense dirt. They assembled a team of world-class engineers and material scientists and got busy creating Lomi. Together, they designed a remarkable, easy-to-use, one-button kitchen appliance that converts food waste into compost.

Company design: Co-founders Matt and Brad were frustrated that governments only made small, incremental improvements to the environment. They wanted to create a movement of for-profit businesses that could make a meaningful dent. So, they harnessed entrepreneurship and technology innovation to help create "a waste-free world." The company raised $7 million via crowdfunding and ultimately attracted investment from superstar Jay-Z. (They also convinced this merry band of Category Pirates to jump on board the ship and help them design this new category. Working with the Lomi team has been a joy.)

Lomi is a certified B Corp, along with companies like Patagonia, Ben & Jerry's, and Seventh Generation. The company says it's "on a mission to leave the planet better than how we found it by eliminating more than 10 billion pounds of waste." (Jim Collins of *Good to Great* fame teaches that legendary companies have these types of "Big Hairy Audacious Goals.")

Matt and Brad developed a powerful direct-to-consumer

business while building an end-to-end supply chain at the same time. Scaling the business has been a meaningful challenge, given that Lomi is one of the fastest-growing new kitchen appliances in a decade. To date, Lomi users have prevented up to seventeen million pounds of food waste from entering the landfill. As a result, many of the top retailers began banging on the company's door.

Category design: Between 40 percent to 50 percent of food gets thrown away. This food waste is responsible for about 22 percent of landfill garbage and produces the annual CO_2 emissions of 42 coal-fired power plants. On top of that, food waste is gross. Dragging a wet, dripping, saggy trash bag out of the kitchen and into the garbage bin is messy and disgusting.

To tackle this problem, Lomi launched a POV video that starts by asking, "What if changing the world was as easy as pushing a button?" The company's launch video is a perfect blend of category POV and product demo. In it, Lomi frames the problem, presents a vision for a different future, and shows how its offering is the solution. As a result of that one video, the Lomi sold out of product for the first nine months it was on the market.

The Lomi founders created a massive new demand from nothing, to solve a problem most people never thought about (food waste) with a "smart home composter." They executed all three sides of the Magic Triangle at once. That's what made Lomi one of the most rapidly growing new kitchen categories in years, with stunning new product revenue—all with $7 million in crowdfunding.

If you are successful at prosecuting all three sides of the Magic Triangle, you will unlock a company's most valuable asset: your data flywheel.

Data flywheels are how you can anticipate the direction of future headwinds and tailwinds.

Data is the culmination of insights you capture from your **category, customers, competition**, and your **opportunistic lens** on how to best use those insights to expand your category, create a new category, and/or partner with other companies to achieve one of these two outcomes. Once you capture the data, your flywheel goes round and round.

1. A breakthrough product combined with an innovative business model, framed within a new and different future for the customer/consumer/user has the highest likelihood of becoming a Category Queen.

2. Once a Category Queen is established, data accumulation creates an "unfair advantage" for the company.

3. This "unfair advantage" means the Category Queen is best positioned to take advantage of the next "category creation" opportunity.

And so on, and so forth.

The purpose of the data flywheel is not to capture data for data's sake. Customer flywheel information can also be "training data" for artificial intelligence (AI). Any company that has rich data stores about customers, products, and revenue can now let AI loose on that data to provide insights and drive actions like never before, thanks to AI and its countless use case applications.

The purpose of your data flywheel is to better educate, market to, and serve your Superconsumers. This fuels profitability, which drives continued customer and data acquisition. This allows you to better anticipate the next compelling category worth creating and maintain your leadership position in the category.

Now, let's tie this all together.

Category Design is the Single Point of Failure in the Magic Triangle

Every company faces three risks when forging its way in the world:

1. **Execution risk:** "Can we create a meaningful product in the time frame that matters?"

2. **Competition risk:** "Are we the team and business capable of winning the category battle?"

3. **Category risk:** "Are we naming and claiming the category wherein we are the undisputed King or Queen?"

However, when it comes to prosecuting the Magic Triangle, there is only one point of failure. You can get the product wrong and tweak it over time. You can get the company/ team/business model wrong and tweak it over time.

If you get the category wrong, you're finished.

- No food delivery, no DoorDash

- No sustainable energy, no Tesla
- No food composting, no Lomi

The big question is, "How do you make sure the category is correct?"

What Lululemon teaches us about the Magic Triangle

(Hint: It's not a yoga pose.)

Lululemon's rise to stardom isn't just about crafting stretchy pants. It's about nailing the Magic Triangle and proving that without a category, you're toast. Lululemon has stumbled multiple times with its company and products, and it was the mighty athleisure category that saved the company's chakras.

- **Product design:** Lululemon didn't just create clothes—it designed a new category of innovative, stylish, and functional athletic wear. It made the smart decision to name its leggings (old category) something different. Its luxury fabrics and premium pricing set the bar high, forcing everyone else to play catch-up. And when it hit a bump in 2013 with the yoga pants recall (a product fail), what happened? The power of the athleisure category and Lululemon's Category Queen status saved the day, letting the company bounce back stronger than ever.

- **Company design:** Lululemon has a clear category vision, a focused culture, and a no-nonsense approach to execution. But as a public company, they've had several erratic moments and disappointed investors.

- **Category design:** This side is where Lululemon's tale becomes legendary. It created a category and ignited a revolution. By designing and driving the athleisure wave, Lululemon took its place as the leader in the athleisure space. Even when it faltered, the sheer strength of the category it had created acted as a lifeline and pulled the company back from the brink of failure.

Lululemon reported a net revenue of $8.1 billion in 2022, a 29.6 percent increase from 2021. In 2023, the company had a $50 billion market cap. Why such a premium? The athleisure category was valued at $155 billion in 2018 and is expected to reach $257 billion by 2026. Lululemon is the undisputed Category Queen, so it earns the majority of the category's value.

The moral of the Lululemon story?

Your category is your single point of failure.

You can trip up on the company or product fronts, but if you lose your grip on the category—poof. You're done. Lululemon's success shows that the ultimate key to winning in business is to dominate the category you create.

Having a category to market yourself within, in addition to a breakthrough product and company design, allows you to separate yourself further and further from any and all competition. This creates the perception of being irreplaceable. That's the "magic" of the Magic Triangle.

But before you dive too deep, you have to get to know your ideal customer—a Superconsumer.

Build for Your Superconsumer, Not Every Consumer

A "Super" is the kind of person who knows your category better than anyone else—oftentimes, even better than you do.

Superconsumers can help point to breakthrough opportunities, hiding in plain sight.

Supers are the consumers pushing the category forward. They are receptive to the new. They are looking for "different." And if you can get even 1 percent of the Supers in the top 10 percent of consumers in the category connected to your new and different future, you'll become the Category King. Your Supers will tell other Supers. And so on, and so on...

Here's why, in the discipline of category design, you want to build for your Superconsumers.

The Power of Superconsumers

The biggest benefit of Superconsumers comes down to simple math. Pound for pound, Supers generate the most power in a category. They're the first to spot breakthrough products and business-model innovations—and they are quick to point out their frustrations with current category offerings. In fact, Supers leave so many digital breadcrumbs, that if you see anyone commenting extensively about a category on social media, an online review, or a Reddit forum, it's 99 percent likely they are a Superconsumer.

We all have friends who are Supers:

- The winos who arrive for a casual night of drinks with seven types of wine glasses
- The self-help readers who own every book in the genre
- The sound engineers who collect studio amps and vintage microphones

Though Supers are few in number—usually about 10 percent of consumers for a particular product or category (not 10 percent of your customers)—they can drive between 30 percent and 70 percent of sales, an even greater share of category profit, and 100 percent of the insights. And yet, when it comes to building companies, launching products, and creating new categories, Supers are almost always a forgotten piece of the puzzle.

If you want to make sure you are innovating in the right direction, go talk to your Supers.

It's the quickest way to find clarity and understand why

the smartest decision you'll ever make as an entrepreneur, marketer, investor, or creator is building for *them*. Why? Because Superconsumers are:

- **Emotional buyers who base their purchase decisions on their life aspirations.** The products they buy represent their love and identity attachment to the category.

- *Not* **price sensitive.** They have emotional and aspirational connections to the products they love and are usually willing to spend more overall *and* pay a higher average price per unit.

- **More predictable than other consumers.** The root cause of their behaviors is deep emotions and motivations, rather than socioeconomics or demographics.

- **Willing to offer wisdom and new insights about product potential within the category.** They are the ones most intimately familiar with all the current product options out there.

- **Most likely to introduce potential Supers to your new category of product.** Potential Supers represent 20 percent of a category's consumer base and respond well to the same advertising, marketing, and product innovations that Supers do.

Instead of asking all of your customers what they think of your product or service (resulting in a mixed bag of contradictory feedback), focus on building relationships with the 10 percent who live and breathe your category of product (not just the top 10 percent of your customers).

Now, grab yourself a rum, and meet us in the hull of the ship. We've got a pirate tale for you.

Southwest, the world's largest low-cost carrier airline, was started by one of our favorite pirates of all time—Herb Kelleher.

At first, his focus was narrow.

In 1967, Southwest started as an intrastate airline solely within the state of Texas. Planes would fly between Dallas, Houston, and San Antonio—and that was it. They kept costs low by flying the Boeing 737, serving peanuts, and operating out of less-expensive secondary airports.

As a result, Southwest started turning a profit in 1973 and didn't suffer a money-losing year until the COVID pandemic in 2020.

So how did Kelleher arrive at this breakthrough idea?

He found underserved, ignored Supers by looking in places other airlines failed to look. Southwest Supers weren't "airline supers" because, as we know, airline consumers in the '60s, '70s, and '80s were a very different group of travelers. They had the means to fly across the country. They expected comfort in the sky.

But those weren't the flyers Southwest focused on serving.

Instead, Southwest focused on giving people in Texas—who otherwise would have to drive four and a half hours from Dallas to San Antonio—the ability to get there in a quarter of the time for a fraction of the cost. Their Supers weren't actually in the "airline" category. Their Supers were in the "road trip" category.

So, Southwest wasn't really in the airline business. It was in the "you are now free to move about the country" business. You can hear this in the Languaging Kelleher used in one of Southwest's first television commercials, "We want our customers to spend their time in the air, not on the ground."

Fifty years later, Southwest Airlines remains the Category Queen of low-cost air travel.

That's the power of Superconsumers.

We feel strongly about not just talking to your category Supers but treating them as collaborators. Talking to your supers will give you the clarity and insight needed to prosecute all three sides of the Magic Triangle. All of this said, if you want to design a new and different category, you can't expect Superconsumers to just give you the answer. They know a lot about where they are (in the context of their category). And they have a pretty good idea of where they would like to be or what they would like more of (and would be willing to pay a premium for as a result). But they usually can't fill in the middle.

Superconsumers cannot design a breakthrough category on their own.

That's your job.

You're responsible for discovering who your Superconsumers are and finding both the analog and digital breadcrumbs they leave behind that tell you where they've been and where they will go next.

To understand your Superconsumers, ask the following types of questions using an array of data lenses:

1. **Microscope questions:**
   - Where do they spend their money in the category?
   - How do they spend their time in the category?
   - How do they spend their emotions, energy, and reputation? What do they care about and why?
   - What are the whys (go seven "whys" deep at least) behind the buys?
   - How did they become a Super? What is their origin story?

2. **Telescope questions:**
   - Given all of the above, where are they likely to spend their money, time, emotions, energy, and reputation?
   - Where did they just come from, and where are they going?
   - How does their behavior fit into a larger life quest/mission?

3. **Wide-angle lens questions:**
   - Where else are they also "Super?"
   - Who else has a relationship with my Supers?
   - Who else wants to join their quest and mission?

4. **Mirror questions:**
   - Can I credibly play a role to help them on their quest?

- How else can I help them?
- Is their mission more important than my success?

These are different questions than what most legacy businesses typically want to know, like gender, age, income, and so on. Demographic questions can be helpful in painting the picture around the edges, but demographics aren't that predictive of category-specific behavior. Instead, questions like these can help you pinpoint *who within your massive dataset of customers* are the ones you should spend the vast majority of your time, energy, resources, and attention serving.

If you can get even 1 percent of the Supers in the top 10 percent of consumers in the category connected to your new and different future, the fight is over. You win.

A big part of winning is understanding where your Supers are and what else attracts their interest.

A Superconsumer of One Category Is a Superconsumer of Nine Categories

When it comes to building companies, launching products, and creating new categories, Supers are almost always a forgotten piece of the puzzle.

Superconsumers know your category better than anyone else.

These people go beyond mere consumers. They possess an unwavering passion for a particular product, brand, or category of goods and services. Their consumption habits are remarkable—constantly making purchases, showing brand loyalty, and not hesitating to splurge on top-notch quality or exclusive offerings. They are true aficionados. And they can unlock exponential growth for your business in adjacent categories.

For example, if you're a movie Superconsumer, you're also probably a Superconsumer of:

- Movie snacks like popcorn and candy
- Home theater equipment
- Expandable pants
- Exclusive behind-the-scenes content
- Vintage movie posters and memorabilia
- And so on

What doesn't get talked about enough is how powerful Superconsumers can be in unlocking exponential growth for your business in adjacent categories. Or even *not so seemingly* adjacent categories. The reason is because a Super of one category is also a Super of up to nine other categories as well.

Once you understand this, you can see different categories and opportunities worth exploring.

This is a wallet share game, not a market share game.

- Wallet share is about capturing more spending *per customer.*
- Market share is about capturing more spending *in the category.*

If you're a math-minded person, think of Supers as the ultimate expression of lifetime value. The lifetime value equation often has these variables:

1. Frequency of purchase... *Supers buy a lot and often!*

2. Average gross margin per purchase... *Supers are willing to pay a premium.*

3. Years in the category... *Supers have the highest category lifespan.*

4. Churn/retention rate... *This is very low at the category level for Supers.*

5. Word of mouth... *This is exponentially higher for Supers, who are the best evangelists.*

6. Categories cross-sold... *Super of one equals Super of nine categories.*

Most companies go through the first four variables. Less go through the last two. This is where the Superconsumer drives the most value but is often the least measured. Done correctly, you acquire a Superconsumer once and you monetize them nine times in different categories.

The signal for customer profitability and sales and marketing efficiency is LTV/CAC.

Lifetime value of the customer divided by customer acquisition cost.

When you prioritize spending the lion's share of your efforts and resources educating and marketing to your Superconsumers, the lifetime value of your customers goes up (because your Supers spend more with you, more often) while simultaneously bringing your customer acquisition cost down. (You've found your Supers. Now you just need to give them more things to get excited about).

Numerator goes up. Denominator goes down.

When you do this successfully, that's *money*.

When you decide to focus on wallet share instead of market share, suddenly, you aren't competing. You're focused on creating. Expanding. Growing. You're focused on finding and evangelizing your Supers, meaning your competition is irrelevant. Because if you understand that a Super of one is also a Super of nine other categories, then you can see revenue.

You can see the new and different categories worth exploring.

Exercise: How to Find Your Supers and the Nine Other Categories They Are Also (Probably) Interested In

Start by asking yourself these eight questions:

1. Who?

Every Superconsumer has an origin story.

- "Why am I a health nut? My dad had a heart attack, and I want to avoid that for myself."
- "Why am I a watch collector? My mom used to repair watches in our garage, and I'd sit and help her every day after school."
- "Why am I a Bitcoin believer? My family lost everything in the 2008 housing crisis, so I don't trust the banking system."
- "Why am I an engineer? My mom worked at IBM, and she used to take me to work, where I became fascinated by computers."

The origin stories of your Supers is incredibly important, if for no other reason than to help you stop seeing this person as a customer (a buying unit you think of transactionally) and start seeing them as a loyal, emotional, highly intelligent enthusiast of the types of products and/or services you hope to create in the world. More tactically, when you understand how your Supers became who they are, you will also understand their drivers, their aspirations, and why they care so deeply about whatever it is they're a Super of.

After all, you can't see the full category constellation Superconsumers have unless you also have deep empathy for the desires, aspirations, and life quests that drive them in the first place.

2. Where?

The most effective way to find where your Supers hang out is by converting your customer data into a per capita metric by zip code. (These are the Super-Geos we mentioned in Law #2 and explain how to find in Law #22.)

No data is more powerful for your business than finding local regions with clusters of your Supers. For example, a while back, Ben & Jerry's discovered that three thousand grocery stores (greater than 10 percent) drove half the sales of all Cherry Garcia SKUs. That meant that advertising in 90 percent of grocery stores in America was largely a waste of money.

Or let's say you're a startup trying to figure out where to launch your Lightning Strike (a marketing strategy we cover in Law #20). Wouldn't it be helpful to launch your startup in a local area that is hot and heavy with Superconsumers?

If you can take the data you have and localize it, all of a sudden, you have context as to why people are behaving the way they are based on proximity.

3. When?

Who and *where* are the lowest hanging fruit to find. *When* is *literally talking about what season, month, week, day, time of day, and second* Supers shop compared to the rest of the consumers in the category. *When* is also a great place to hunt for Supers—however this can be a heavily analytic exercise.

When is literally the season, month, week, day, time of day, and second Supers shop compared to the rest of the category.

This matters because an incredible amount of conventional wisdom can be overturned here.

For example, the conventional wisdom for sparkling wine is that the holidays (Christmas and New Year's Eve) are the peak times to sell. Every company and brand of sparkling wine then spends most of their marketing and promotion dollars there—and ends up in a race to the bottom as a result. What goes unnoticed in the sparkling wine category is that Supers also buy surplus amounts on other holidays, notably Memorial Day until Labor Day.

That's because Supers are the queens of incremental, clever use cases for the category.

And sparkling wine Supers are consumers who love cold, refreshing, bubbly alcoholic drinks—*for any occasion*. Said differently, they swap out beer for sparkling wine whenever possible. Understanding *when* Supers buy can deliver a tremendous amount of operating profit, simply by targeting Supers during low seasonal periods when a company may not be covering fixed costs and avoiding high seasons where no one makes profit. This is where technology can start to add fuel to the fire. Some of the most sophisticated marketers use marketing mix modeling and multi-touch attribution analysis to figure out when their Supers buy and when other companies are quiet.

All of that said, artificial intelligence and machine learning aren't great at understanding *who* your Supers are (origin story) or even *where* they are (Super-Geos). These are insights that have to be extracted from the data, not just the data itself. But once you have these insights, now you can tell technology which direction you'd like it to keep exploring and learning.

This is what answers the important question of *"when?"* When are our Supers doing what they're doing? Is there a time of year they're most active? Is there a moment when they're most likely to make a purchase? When in the year, quarter, month, week, day, second, should we be marketing to them?"

4. How?

Understanding how your Supers behave is paramount to understanding how to maximize lifetime customer value and happiness.

- Do your Supers prefer subscribing monthly? Do they buy yearly?
- Do they pay with credit card? Cash? Direct deposit?
- Do they need to talk to someone in advance? How many touch points are required for them to convert?
- What pricing tier/package are they most likely to start with? What's the path for them to rise up the value chain?
- How many purchase something additional after just one month? Three months? A year?

These are the sorts of questions that help you understand which points of friction in your business are most important to solve first. Because the less friction there is, specifically for your Supers, the faster you are going to grow revenues—because again, your Supers are the ones spending 30 percent to 70 percent more than other less enthusiastic customers.

For example, Amazon spends a considerable amount of time, money, and energy on continuously improving its return process. This is antithetical to the way many company leaders think. But Amazon understands that if returns are easy, the number one barrier for potential eCommerce Supers is removed.

Understanding the "shopping mission" is critical to unearthing the real reason why Supers buy whatever it is they buy. Imagine a Superconsumer buys five Apple TVs yet only has two TVs in their household. How does that make sense? Well, what most companies don't realize is that Supers are great gifters. They love the category so much they are often gifting it to other people they love. The other three Apple TVs were gifts to friends and family.

Unfortunately, this purchasing behavior tends to get labeled as "strange" or even "extreme," leaving most companies to neither understand nor utilize this as a strategy.

5. What Else?

Here's where things start getting fun.

What else are your Supers interested in? More specifically, if you know the nine categories the Supers are Supers in, what might be the tenth category that has yet to be created? These questions become infinitely easier to answer once you've taken the time to gather data and insights from the preceding questions. This is easier if you understand the following:

- Various Supers' origin stories
- A sense of where the Super-Geos are located
- A working understanding of *when* and *how* your Supers purchase and interact with their favorite products

Once you have this context, you can productively ask the question, "So, what else does this Superconsumer want? What else would they be interested in, appreciate, and become excited about?" This is the difference between optimizing for wallet share vs. market share.

More importantly, this is how you design a new category breakthrough.

6. Why?

Once you understand why, you have a category

breakthrough on your hands.

For example, Honda Civics sell like crazy in Southern California. Why? Because customers trick them out like the cars in The Fast and the Furious movies. Understanding this *why* is crucial because, if you're Honda, wouldn't it be smart to tap into that Superconsumer behavior?

Instead of these Supers hiding away in the shadows, why not evangelize them?

- Why not make their enthusiasm known to attract other Supers?

- Why not launch the Super Civic, which is nothing but the base-level Honda Civic except with hundreds of LEGO-like attachments and cosmetic additions you can purchase to build your car into your own unique expression?

- Why not create an XGames-like Super Civic event? Or a YouTube version of Pimp My Ride called "Pimp My Civic," and celebrate the tuners who work on their cars?

Or maybe (paying attention to the *when*), you learn your Supers would actually prefer to pay a monthly subscription renting cosmetic parts instead of buying parts outright— unlocking a whole new recurring revenue stream for the business.

To answer this question, ask yourself, "Why do your Supers do what they do? Why do they get excited about whatever it is they get excited about? Why do they love what they love?"

7. How Much?

Is there a ceiling? If so, how much?

What's incredible about Superconsumers is that if you can tap into their wants, needs, and desires, you'll discover they are willing to pay a premo-premium for the things they just can't get enough of. For example, a regular consumer of scissors might only spend five dollars in the category over the course of a few years. But a Superconsumer of scissors, someone who loves scrapbooking or home projects, might spend upwards of a hundred dollars on scissors—maybe even a hundred dollars per month, multiple months out of the year (scissors with different handles and lengths, scissors for different projects, etc.).

When you evaluate your product or service through the lens of all customers ("What is the average person willing to pay for this?"), you end up underpricing your offerings and undervaluing your Supers.

For example, YETI proved you could create Superconsumers for outdoor coolers—a category that had largely been undervalued as little more than a big plastic container that keeps stuff cold. Before YETI, people would buy a Coleman for $75 to $125 dollars. And so when YETI started charging a thousand dollars per outdoor cooler, they framed a new level of value in the "premium cooler" category they designed.

What do your Supers find most valuable, and how much would they be willing to spend for that delight?

They'll pay accordingly.

8. What Next?

All of these questions, together, create your data flywheel.

A Super of one is also a Super of nine. Those nine other tangential interests/categories are fruitful partnerships worth being explored and opportunities for new and different category breakthroughs to occur. Which means the more deeply you understand your Supers, and the more data you have about *where, when, how,* and *why* they do what they do, the easier it will be for you to spot the tenth category that doesn't yet exist.

Without your Supers, you are just another company churning and burning away, accelerating your customer acquisition costs but not actually increasing the lifetime value of your customers.

Supers are not just the key for unlocking category potential in one category. Supers can actually help point to new vistas of opportunity and breakthrough ideas hiding in plain sight. But without the category lens, most people can't see them.

How to apply that category lens is up next.

Part 2

CATEGORY

Category First, Brand Second

Success is your ability to create a new and differentiated category of product, service, or offering to which your brand name just happens to be attached.

It's shocking how many MBAs, entrepreneurs, founders, and smart investors prioritize the brand *before* the category. They focus on our name. Our logo. Our team. Our "mission statement."

(As if customers care about us... how arrogant.)

That is why you get twenty thousand results when you type "branding books" into Amazon. While we haven't read all of them, we've read many of the most important ones. And virtually all of them say that building a brand is critical to building a successful business. We ask you to consider that they are wrong.

Just think for a second, and consider something… different.

Brands are often described as "solutions."

Well, the entire brand marketing work missed the fact that no one buys a solution unless they have a problem. Said in a different way, drill buyers don't buy drills. They actually buy holes. But drill manufacturers yell "my drill!" without considering that the customer only cares about *their holes*.

Brands are about us, but categories are about customers, consumers, clients, and subscribers. If you put the category first, you prioritize these people's problems, wants, and needs. Category Kings win by putting the customers' problems first.

Market your brand, and I think you want my money. Market my problem, and I think you want to help me.

Categories make brands, not the other way around.

- Brand marketing is something we do *to* customers.
- Category marketing is something we do *for* customers.

We know this is a hard concept for many marketing people to "get" because unlearning is way harder than learning. The thing is, legendary entrepreneurs and innovators don't design just brands. They design new categories for their breakthrough products and business models to live within.

Take a moment to consider the following examples:

- No crowdfunding, no GoFundMe
- No online dating, no Tinder
- No generative AI, no OpenAI
- No e-commerce, no Amazon

Before you even think about branding, your company needs a category to market itself within.

This idea has become terribly misunderstood over the years, so let us clarify. You *do not* want to market within an *existing* market. Instead, you want to create a *new* and *different* category that you have free reign to market *within*. And yet, many people continue to put the brand before the category. Some people even think brands make categories.

If that were true, we would be taking pictures on Kodak smartphones, renting homes from Marriott, and buying electric vehicles from GM.

Ask any person on earth why Ralph Lauren was successful, for example, and 99 percent of them will say the same thing: "He built an incredible brand." But is that actually what *caused* his success?

Or was the Ralph Lauren brand the result of creating a *different* category?

Most people don't know that Ralph Lauren is credited with creating the menswear industry as "a designer reality." In the 1960s, men had gotten used to prescriptive dressing and wore suits as uniforms with very little differentiation and personality. "Designers were for the women. The tailor was for men." Lauren was the first *designer* to turn American "lifestyle" moments and characters (a carpenter, a railroad worker, a cowboy) into fashionable, everyday looks.

And it all started with his unique "wide" ties.

He designed the first tie to break the mold of what a tie should look like for men—and the first tie that even remotely resembled having its own distinct style. Ralph's ties were *different*. As a result, he created a new category of *wide designer* ties. The "brand" and the tag simply let people know where they could get more *different* ties like it.

And in the 1960s, what happens when you wear a wide tie?

Well, you need different shirts with different collars. You need a different suit. (New categories create more new categories.) And suddenly, Ralph Lauren was creating a whole new category of menswear. What Lauren was *not* doing was copying and pasting his brand onto similar commodity products. He was inventing new and *different* products— which, after the fact, were paired with the Ralph Lauren tag and brand.

Our guess is that many people extol the value of "building a brand" as a path to success (not understanding that the category made the brand).

Much "marketing thinking" is heavy on the marketing and light on the thinking.

(Harsh, but true.)

A case in point is Liquid Death, the canned water company. Most people say this beverage company succeeded because it did a great job at branding. Yes, that's true. But Liquid Death did not win the category because it had a "cool" logo and "vibe" (although it did). It won the category because of category design.

In 2023, Liquid Death was the most followed beverage brand in the U.S. on TikTok because it designed a new category: canned water.

The company called bullshit on the "plastic bottled water category" and proclaimed that cans are recyclable in a way plastic is not, with a simple message, "Death to plastic." Liquid Death did not compete with Evian water. Everything about Liquid Death was different, not better—including the category.

Canned water was different.

Unfortunately, too many companies believe that sprinkling some kind of magic dust on their "brand" (changing the colors, the font, the logo design, etc.) is going to drive a breakthrough in growth. Or even worse, they say, "Let's use big, all-encompassing, undifferentiated language to make ourselves appeal to everyone. Something like, 'We are an authentic, purpose-driven brand.'"

We will live the rest of our lives wondering how branding is a "solution" to a lack of differentiation.

You will never overthrow the category leader by extending your brand into someone else's category.

Yet brand marketers do this all the time.

In 2009, one of the most well-known brands in the world, Microsoft, decided to take on Apple's legendary in-store customer experience by launching the Microsoft Store. By 2015, the company announced, "More than 80 percent of Americans live within 20 miles of a Microsoft store, with more than 110 stores across the U.S., Puerto Rico, and Canada."

Fast-forward to 2020, and Microsoft decided to shut the doors on the operation, "resulting in a pre-tax charge of approximately $450 million." That's half a billion dollars spent trying to extend their brand into Apple's category. A CNBC article summed up the extent of this brand-extending attempt, "Microsoft even built a store on 5th Avenue in New York City, just blocks away from Apple's iconic glass cube store."

The lesson here: You can't take your brand and stroll up into someone else's category.

The Powerful Role of Brands in Category Design

If branding doesn't work, what's a marketer, an executive, or an entrepreneur to do?

The answer is certainly not to come up with airy-fairy attributes in an attempt to "distinguish" the company, product, or service from identical offerings. Branding in the absence of category design is asinine. Instead, branding should be used in conjunction *with the new and different category you are creating.*

For example, Google's brand is only valuable in the context

of the category it created and dominated—the "search" category. Take Google's brand and extend it into Facebook's "social network" category, and it's worthless. The same goes for Microsoft and its attempt to extend its brand into Apple's category of in-store experiences. (Remember: Categories make brands, not the other way around.)

As a category designer, it's your responsibility to make the category and brand come together in a meaningful way for the customer, consumer, or user.

Here are a few examples:

- **Bombas:** The category is socks, but the brand is about a commitment to comfort, performance, and social impact. The company focuses on thoughtful design, high-quality materials, and a donation program for homeless individuals. In fact, the name Bombas is derived from the Latin word for bumblebee, an animal that works together for the greater good of the hive. That's why the company's logo is a bee and its slogan is "Bee Better."

- **5-Hour Energy:** It's not an energy drink—it's an energy shot. Both the category and brand reflect a convenient, effective, and fast-acting alternative to traditional energy drinks. 5-Hour Energy's brand centers on the "no crash" promise, a variety of flavors and formulas for different needs and preferences, and a portable bottle design that works for busy and active consumers. It's a different product, in a different category.

- **Lemonade:** The category is home and renters insurance, which isn't obvious at first. But the brand reflects a different approach to insurance that emphasizes transparency, simplicity, and giving back. With Lemonade, users can get a quote and purchase insurance in minutes, and the company donates any unclaimed premiums to nonprofits chosen by its customers. It's a new and different business model within the insurance category. And the brand makes it clear what will happen when life hands you lemons.

- **Microsoft Bing/ChatGPT:** It's not a "better" search—it's a new category called "answer." It's different. With ChatGPT, users can communicate with a virtual assistant, a chatbot, or another AI-powered tool in a more natural and intuitive way. Everything about it begs the question, "Why search, when you can just get the answer?"

- **Lomi:** The category is composting, but the Lomi brand reflects a convenient, high-tech, and eco-friendly alternative to traditional home composting methods. With the composter, users can turn food waste into nutrient-rich compost in just a few hours, all from the comfort of their own homes. And the brand reflects this different POV. Lomi was named after "loam," a type of soil that is ideal for gardening and agriculture. (In fact, we believe this category has massive potential. So Category Pirates are advisors for and investors in Lomi.)

When you create a meaningful experience for customers, your company's branding efforts create the style guide for the category. You can see this happening when competitors start talking like you, looking like you, and building similar features as you. For example, the same week Clari—a revenue operations platform—launched its expanded Revenue Platform category, competitors began ripping off the company's unique Revenue Collaboration and Governance point of view. (As advisors with behind-the-scenes access to Clari's marketing, it was wild to watch people steal the company's exact Languaging within days of its marketing Lightning Strike!)

Copycats are exactly what you want.

The more companies talk about your category, the more likely it takes off. This is exactly what happened when the insurance incumbent Liberty Mutual tried to mimic Lemonade by launching Lulo. Lemonade tastefully noted the rip-off in a company blog post:

> *Lulo is a shameless doppelgänger of Lemonade, copying our pricing, wording, font, iconography, name, look, feel, and messaging… Liberty Mutual is an incredible company, and it was a little awkward seeing them stoop to selling a Lemonade-facsimile. As you might expect, these efforts produced a lemon, and Liberty quietly deep-sixed Lulo a short while later.*

Copycats make the category bigger. As the category leader, copycats will only help you capture the lion's share of the economics. (Remember: 76 percent of the entire category.) So, if you are an entrepreneur, an executive, or a marketer, we urge you to ask this very important question:

What are you *doing* with your marketing?

- Are you inviting a comparison? *"We're like everybody else, BUT better."*

- Or are you forcing a choice? *"We are a different thing altogether."*

The answer to this question is the seminal difference between brand marketing and category marketing. A majority of marketing actually invites the customer to compare. It says, "We have six mega flops, and our next nearest competitor has four."

This is an insane strategy.

Exercise: Put Your Category First and Your Brand Second

Do you truly believe the category is first and the brand second? Do you act and lead that way? If you're unsure of where you stand, we encourage you to ask yourself the following questions.

1. What emotions do you feel when another brand in your category does something amazing (breakthrough innovation, clever business-model shift, marketplace win, etc.)? Do you feel happy, joyful, angry, or jealous? Write down the top emotions you feel. Be honest.

   ➤ _____

   ➤ _____

   ➤ _____

   ➤ _____

   ➤ _____

2. Think about your budget for this current fiscal year. What percent of it is focused mostly on your brand/company or on the category? Is it more than 50 percent on your brand? Is it more than 75 percent? 90 percent? Write down the number and date it.

Today

Budget: _____ as of __ __ / __ __ / __ __ __ __

- _____ percent of your brand/company
- _____ percent of your category

Come back and write the amounts again in three months, six months, and one year.

Three-Month Mark

Budget: _____ as of __ __ / __ __ / __ __ __ __

- _____ percent of your brand/company
- _____ percent of your category

Six-Month Mark

Budget: _____ as of __ __ / __ __ / __ __ __ __

- _____ percent of your brand/company
- _____ percent of your category

One-Year Mark

Budget: _____ as of __ __ / __ __ / __ __ __ __

- _____ percent of your brand/company
- _____ percent of your category

3. Charlie Munger famously said, "Show me the incentive, and I'll show you the outcome." To understand your incentives, look at your key performance indicators, dashboards, and key business metrics. Think about your incentive plans for your bonuses, options vesting, promotions, or other compensation or career advancement. Write down the top key performance indicators and metrics that have the greatest impact.

_____

(Brand Performance / Category Performance)

_____

(Brand Performance / Category Performance)

_____

(Brand Performance / Category Performance)

_____

(Brand Performance / Category Performance)

_____

(Brand Performance / Category Performance)

How many of these metrics measure your brand or company's performance vs. the category's performance? Circle the answer next to each metric.

4. Look at your latest sales brochure, product manual, marketing copy, or website. Read the first paragraph, and organize the words/phrases you see into the following buckets:

- Category _____
- Customer Problem _____

- Customer Value   _____
- Your POV   _____
- Your Company   _____
- Your Brand   _____
- Your Product/Offer   _____

Do you have more words in the top half or the bottom half of the buckets? The top three buckets put your category first, and the bottom four buckets put your brand first.

5. Most companies have a thirty-second elevator pitch for their product or brand. Do you have a thirty-second elevator pitch for your category? If you do, write it below. If you don't have one, take a few minutes to write a first draft.

_____

_____

_____

_____

How compelling is your pitch? Would you share this with your closest loved ones (mom, kids, best friend) and feel great? Or are you embarrassed, squeamish, or reluctant in any way? Are you in love with your category? Why or why not?

Category designers do not want to be compared to others. They want all others to be compared to them.

Somehow, the business world got duped into solving a problem called "We're Not Different" by putting branding drapes on the painting instead of creating a different painting. Stop arguing over whose drapes are the best. Instead, paint a *different* painting.

The next chapter explains how to go about it.

Position Yourself or Be Positioned

If you are comparable, you are replaceable.

Being a successful category designer requires some immeasurable combination of hard work, luck, and commitment to something *bigger* than yourself.

Fortunately, you can do this at any stage of life if you position yourself well and niche down. Unfortunately, the goal for many creators and companies is to be known—and to be known by lots of people. The thinking here is once you have people's attention, you can then decide what to do with it (aka, make money). But to what end? And at what cost?

There is a cost, so we're going to explain the issues with "personal branding" and share a Pirate-approved alternative called personal category design.

Too often, building a "personal brand" turns your entire content strategy into an exercise in talking about you.

"Hey, guys! It's me. Uh, just another day. I'm having a burrito for breakfast. LOL!"

Your "personal brand" is a distraction at best and a self-inflicted wound at worst. And depending on what kind of quote graphics you've been puking out as of late, it may even be cause for medical attention. This is why you want to avoid personal branding and focus on personal category design.

Personal Category Design is your Commitment to Something Bigger than Yourself.

It can take on a variety of forms:

- You become known for discussing a specific type of subject matter.
- You become known for creating a new and differentiated genre.
- You become known for unlocking a rare and valued result.
- You become known for facilitating a certain kind of change.

To "become known for a new and differentiated niche you own," start by asking: Who would your Superconsumers say you are? Reputations are *earned* by the category, the customers, and the ecosystem around you.

The reason Pirate Christopher is who he is, is because legendary Silicon Valley venture capitalists, founders, and executives say who he is. Not because he contrived a brand.

The reason Pirate Eddie is who he is, is because legendary S&P 500 executives and elite business thinkers say who he is. Not because he contrived a brand.

The reason Pirate Cole is who he is, is because millions of readers on the Internet say who he is. Not because he contrived a brand.

The reason Pirate Katrina is who she is, is because a legendary network of editors, writers, and entrepreneurs say who she is. Not because she contrived a brand.

Personal category design works. It has worked for all four of us. It has worked for our friends, family members, and colleagues who we care deeply for and want to help live with as much agency and financial independence as possible. And we know it will work for you.

Here's what it takes to position yourself to serve others in a meaningful and valuable way.

Step 1: Get in the game and start creating categories.

Start small with this simple equation: *You do X for Y because you want to solve Z.*

For example, you help musicians (X) turn their songs into NFTs (Y) because you believe artists should be fairly compensated for their music and blockchain technology is a step in that direction (Z). Notice how the X and Y variables of the equation *are about other people* (and more importantly, a specific group/category of person), and the Z variable of the equation is both your POV of the category (why it matters) and/or your personal story (why it matters to you).

But your personal story, or even who you are, is *not* the main character.

The *reader, the listener, the customer, the user* is the main character—and the degree to which you can educate and delight *them* on this new and differentiated category you are creating dictates the degree to which they will care about "you." Because the truth is, the hero in everyone's movie is themselves. So even when people "care about you," the reality is they care about *how you make them feel* a whole lot more.

Even when it looks like it's about you, it's not. It's always about *them*.

And if you are a musician, entrepreneur, creator, innovator, executive, or artist of any kind, it's important to remember that success is *not* about the music you make or the art you produce or the content you create or the cabadingulator you invent or the company you build. It's about how *others feel* about what you did and how they talk about their transformation as a result.

The very best way to learn how to create your own personal category and become known for a niche you own is to get started trying to create new niche categories.

Start small.

One of our favorite examples is My Wedding Songs.

Pirate Matt Campbell, founder of My Wedding Songs, said to Pirate Christopher (after being exposed to category design thinking), "I changed from being a broadline wedding planning website to being the Category King of wedding song suggestions. When the change was made, we saw a hockey stick effect in growth. Instead of trying to be everything to everybody, now we just focus on one thing and try to be great at it. It is also easier to promote something that is so specific. And now, we are seen as the leader of the category we niched down and created."

In a world of billions of digital songs and countless wedding planning services, Matt stands alone. He's incomparable and irreplaceable. He's in a category of one—a snow leopard.

As a rule of thumb: If your niche feels too small, it's probably not small enough.

Whenever you feel the urge to "aim bigger," do the opposite. Dig deeper. Get more and more specific. Create something that feels custom tailored for one specific person—then go find all the other people who would be interested in that exact same thing.

Step 2: Pick a specialty.

Once you get in the game and start creating niche categories, inevitably you will discover (a) where your true interests are and (b) what the market finds most valuable from you.

More specifically, you will start to build relationships with your Superconsumers, and they will start revealing to you a treasure trove of opportunities for compelling personal category design positions. Why? Because Superconsumers always tell the truth about the category: the good, the bad, and the ugly.

- They will tell you what problems they are currently experiencing and what solutions they wish someone would create for them.

- They will tell you what frustrates them about the existing category and what problems they would gladly pay a premium to never experience again.

- They will tell you their wants and needs, hopes and dreams, and signal what would be interesting to them—if only someone would come along and create it, name it, and claim it.

What you're looking for here is: What can you be legendary at that creates significant value for others and that few people can do. Then, frame, name, and claim *that thing*. Once you choose a specialty, how you educate others on the value of this new and different specialty is by creating and managing the value perception gap.

Position yourself, or be positioned.

The highest-paid people on the planet are those who:

1. Solve a problem that is massively valuable to solve

2. Is urgently needed and required to solve (otherwise, bad things happen or continue to happen)

3. And very few other people can solve (making it a rare and not easily replaceable skill set)

Please read these three points several times over, like

a mantra. The entire purpose of choosing a specialty, and naming and claiming your personal category, is to create a value perception gap that is difficult to fill with a commodity (aka, someone other than yourself).

Step 3: Figure out pricing.

Pricing is not a reflection of self-confidence.

This notion that you get paid more in business by puffing out your chest and "faking it until you've made it" is total nonsense. It's harmful thinking (and for category designers, thinking about thinking is the most important kind of thinking).

How you make more money in your business, your career, and your life, is by acquiring skills that widen the value perception gap.

- Want to make $150,000 per year? Well, there are a bunch of real estate agents in the world who make $150,000 per year because they can solve a problem called, "Rich people can't find the right house." If you can acquire the skills to solve that problem, you can make $150,000 too.

- Want to make $300,000 per year? Well, there are a bunch of affiliate marketers on the internet who solve a problem called, "I'm a great innovator and product builder, but I'm terrible at marketing my products." If you can acquire the skills to solve that problem, you can make $300,000 too.

- Want to make $1 billion dollars? Well, there are a bunch of problems in the world like, "How do we get clean water to areas that have no clean water?" If you can acquire the skills to solve that problem (and problems like it), you can become a billionaire too.

Figure out what problems other people value being solved, go acquire those skills, and set your price. However, we'd like to encourage you to take this one step further.

Acquiring a valuable skill is great. But acquiring a valuable skill and positioning that skill within the context of a different problem that you frame, name, and claim unlocks a completely new level of freedom and financial upside.

For example, it's one thing to say, "Real estate agents who sell mansions to rich people can make $150,000 per year or more, and that's what I do." But then you have to duke it out with all the other real estate agents who have acquired those skills, too, and essentially do the exact same thing.

All your time then gets spent trying to convince clients why you're *better, faster, smarter, cheaper* than the competition—risky behavior that, in many cases, forces everyone in the category into a race to the bottom.

You don't want that.

Instead, consider how much more advantageous your position becomes when you say, "Hey, wealthy individuals? The problem you have isn't the problem you think you have. You think what you're looking for is a reliable, trusted real estate agent with a proven track record. And if that's what you're looking for, by all means, go for it. But that's not me.

Who am I? Oh, I'm not a real estate agent. I'm a *Bargain Mansion Hunter.* I do nothing but study all the biggest, most luxurious houses on the market that haven't been sold in over a year, which means they are desperate for an offer and are willing to be sold for way less than asking price. However... I will tell you that these deals are hard to close because people have a hard time letting go of their expensive real estate for below market value. But I've solved that problem, and I know exactly what steps to take to get the deal done for you."

Whoa! That's personal category design!

When you are able to acquire or build a valuable skill *and* frame it in the context of a new and different problem—which you've named and claimed—your ability to charge a premium goes through the roof. Because how else could the customer solve this problem (which you've now taught them is very important to solve) if you're the one who invented/framed the problem?

You're not easily replaceable.

And as a result, you set the price. (To figure out your pricing, jump to Law #15.)

Step 4: Hitch your niche to a rocket ship.

Personal category design plus an intentionally created value perception gap will allow you to charge two times, five times, ten-plus times more than whatever it was you were doing before.

But of course, every industry and category has its ceiling. At a certain point, you can only charge *so much* for an hour of your time. You can only charge *so much* for a book or a course, service, or consulting project.

To get above a ten-time or twenty-time or fifty-time pricing increase, you will likely need to hitch your niche to someone else's rocket ship. This means finding ways to tie your incentives and earnings to someone else's success—who may be playing in a bigger, more highly valued category than you or solving a bigger, even more valuable problem than you. An easy example here would be choosing to take your compensation in stock options as opposed to cash. Maybe you've learned the most you can ever get away with charging a client per month is $20,000 (or $240,000 per year). Anything above that, and they go, "Come on, don't be ridiculous. We're already paying a premium. Let us keep our kidneys, eh?"

How you overcome your theoretical max is by hitching your niche to their rocket ship: "Then how about instead of cash, you give me $240,000 in stock options?"

Here are a few ways you can hitch your niche to a rocket ship:

- Carve out your niche in a category that has twenty-year tailwinds. An abundance of growth covers many sins to allow you to make your mistakes without major repercussions.

- Focus on key inflection points where valuation perceptions change. Pirate Eddie has built $100 million dollar growth strategies for his clients many times. And while they didn't really move the needle for an $80 billion dollar massive company, you better believe it made a monster difference for a $50 million dollar run-rate company looking to go public who wanted to exponentially change its valuation. Change-in-control, M&A transactions, IPOs, or sales are fantastic ways to hitch your niche.

- Take your compensation in stock (in a company you believe in) as opposed to cash.

- Take the cash you generate from your business, services provided, or products sold, and invest it into companies (or Bitcoin) that are solving even bigger, even more valuable problems in the world.

- Tie your incentives to other people's success. For example, some online education programs will teach students at cost/for free then take a portion of their future income based on the new and more lucrative job they're able to get.

The idea here is to change the way your impact is being valued by connecting your upside potential to solving a problem larger than yourself (scaling your value).

The first niche down is scary.

But we want you to know, you can be *different*. All it takes is:

- Getting started
- Choosing a specialty—then framing, naming, and claiming a new and different problem
- Educating others on the value perception gap and charging accordingly
- And eventually, hitching your niche to a rocket ship

This is the treasure map (or at least "a" treasure map!). And once you put it into practice, start small, and begin to see the power of being known for a niche you own, the journey becomes self-evident and deeply satisfying. It keeps you playing the game over and over again. Life becomes more fun. And even if your first personal category design isn't successful (like Pirate Katrina's "custom clay art designer" as a ten-year-old), you will learn and your next one will be an improvement. And so will the one after that.

Eventually, one of them will *hit*, and your life will be completely different as a result.

When you find the one that sticks, you want to frame, name, and claim your unique position and category. The way you do this is by using language that gets people to stop, think, and consider something different.

That's up next.

Whoever Frames the Problem Owns the Solution

Problems create categories, and categories create demand for new solutions.

Category designers have an amazing superpower—they can teach others how to think by the words they use. This is called Languaging, the strategic use of language to create or change thinking. We believe this is one of the most under-discussed, unexamined aspects of business and marketing today.

Why?

A demarcation point in language creates a demarcation point in thinking, which creates a demarcation point in action, which creates a demarcation point in outcome.

Languaging is about creating distinctions between old and new, same and different.

- When the dairy industry spent a hundred years educating the general public that milk comes from cows, then someone came along and introduced Almond Milk, Oat Milk, and Flax Milk, *that's Languaging*.

- When CrossFit popularized a new way of thinking about fitness and workouts by introducing words like "WOD" (Workout of the Day) and "AMRAP" (As Many Rounds as Possible) to set it apart from traditional gym experiences, *that's Languaging*.

- When Slack changed the way people think about workplace communication by introducing terms like "channels" and "workspaces" to streamline communication and collaboration, *that's Languaging*.

The language you use to talk about your new category should make the customer *stop*, tilt their head, and immediately wonder, "This is for something different—do I need this?" It should be clear this thing is not like what came before it. To do that, you have to be the trusted authority on that new language—and subsequently, that new category.

It all starts with how you frame, name, and claim the problem and solution.

Whoever Frames the Problem Owns the Solution

There's a reason why men can have "erectile dysfunction" and not "impotence."

Impotence has very negative implications attached to the word. It implies that someone is "not manly" or "unable to be a man." That's not a word very many men want to be associated with, meaning men don't want to admit to having such a problem. (Hard to sell a solution to a problem no one wants to admit to having!)

In order to solve this problem, Pfizer—the makers of Viagra—*invented a disease* called "erectile dysfunction."

Pfizer made impotence a more approachable problem. Then the company shortened it to "ED" to make it even softer and safer to associate with. It's a whole lot easier for a man to say, "I am experiencing ED" than to say "I am impotent."

Languaging changes the way people perceive the thing they're looking at.

Category designers deliberately use Languaging to frame, name, and claim a solution to differentiate themselves from any and all competition through word choice, tone, and nuance. They use Languaging to speak to (and speak "like") the customers they want to attract, especially the Superconsumers of the category. They use it to further establish their position in the category they are designing or redesigning. And they use it to explain how their company executes all three sides of the Magic Triangle *in a different way.*

Your POV, and the language you use to reflect that POV, makes your "messaging" inspire customers to take action—not the other way around. Let's walk through how you can use Languaging to design a new category.

How to Frame, Name, and Claim a Category

When you invent the language to solve a problem, you become the trusted authority to educate people on the definition of that new language—and subsequently, the definition of that new category. All it takes is a few steps.

Step 1: Frame a different problem or opportunity.

If marketing is your ability to evangelize a new category, and branding is how well you can associate your product with the benefits of the category, then Languaging is how you market the category and your brand within that category, *based on your company's unwavering, unquestionably unique point of view.*

Your POV is what "hooks" the customer by framing a new problem, and your new solution, in a provocative way.

The language you use must reflect your unique point of view.

You can tell when a company doesn't have a unique category POV or Languaging when its "messages" conflict with one another, have unclarified and "weak" aims or, worst of all, have no clear aim at all. Today it's evangelizing one category, and tomorrow it's evangelizing a different category. (This major mistake is often explained as "trying out different marketing and messaging phrases.")

For example, a cereal company might run one advertisement saying, "The healthiest way to start the day!" The very next campaign, however, they might change the message to, "A healthy breakfast alternative." What's the cereal company's unwavering POV of the category?

- Is it that breakfast *is* the best way to start the day and cereal is the solution?

- Or is it that breakfast *isn't* the best way to start the day and cereal is the solution?

Companies with unclarified, undefined POVs eventually conclude that they have a problem (sales are down). But they end up stating the root of their problem in the way they ask for help: "We need to work on our messaging." More times than not, what they mean when they say "messaging" isn't actually *messaging*—it's a category point of view.

Well, how can you possibly know what to say unless you know what you stand for? What difference do you make in the world? What problem do you solve?

Your point of view should be well defined and chiseled into the company's tablets, with intentionally chosen words that reflect the company's POV.

This allows the true science of messaging to begin—a never-ending experiment of swapping in and out of words, phrases, promotions, testimonials, and other "messages" to figure out which are (another very intentional word here) *resonating* and most effectively evangelizing your category POV.

Here are a few unique POV examples from category leaders:

- **Stitch Fix:** Busy people don't have time to shop for clothes, but they want nice clothes that fit their unique style.
- **Vinebox:** Buying an entire bottle of premium wine only to not enjoy what you've just bought is a terrible experience.
- **Netflix:** You should be able to watch anything you want, whenever you want.

You want your POV and the language you use to reflect it to inspire customers to take action.

Step 2: Evangelize a different future.

This step is about standing in a different future and living "as if" that future already exists.

Let's see how the category leaders from above framed the future:

- **Stitch Fix:** Receive curated boxes of clothing, selected just for you by a team of stylists.
- **Vinebox:** Get vials of premium wine by the glass delivered to your door.

- **Netflix:** Instantly "stream" movies and TV shows, instead of waiting for an "appointment viewing" at a set time.

Netflix is a legendary example.

The company's POV is that you should be able to watch anything you want, whenever you want. That's the frame of the problem. It then names and claims the solution to that problem with a new word—streaming.

But Netflix also framed, named, and claimed the *old* category experience too. It did so in a way that was functionally accurate and simultaneously spelled out the immediate problem for customers. Netflix called it "appointment viewing." In order for "streaming" and on-demand to work, you also had to believe "appointment viewing" was a problem. And nobody in the '90s and first decade of the 2000s thought "appointment viewing" was a problem. You just assumed you could only watch what you wanted to watch at the hour it was on. As a result, the language people used back then when asking their friends and family about a new TV show was, "When is it on?"

This phrase, *this language,* no longer exists.

Today, we don't ask, "When is it on?" The new streaming category overtook the old appointment viewing category, which means the new language replaces the old language. We now ask, "What is it on? Netflix? Disney+? HBO? Hulu?" Using language intentionally helps you educate customers on the differences between the new category you are creating and the old category that currently exists.

This leads to the final step.

Step 3: Show customers how your "solution" bridges the gap from the problem or opportunity to a different future.

You are responsible not just for strategically using new words to frame new problems (or reframe old problems) but also for communicating the benefits of your new and different solution. Showing people how your solution bridges the gap to a new, different future helps you highlight the unspoken qualities of your category point of view. In your marketing, branding, and product descriptions, language has the potential to reflect these qualities.

Our friend Lee Hartley Carter, author of *Persuasion: Convincing Others When Facts Don't Seem to Matter*, refers to this as "the understanding that language has the power to create thinking, which in turn inspires action."

Conventional marketing wisdom says, "Market the benefits, not the features." Category design wisdom says, "Market the problem, you become the solution."

For example, when Starbucks customers walk into *any coffee shop other than Starbucks*, what words do they frequently use to order their drinks?

"Hi, I'd like a double grande latte please."

But "grande" isn't the universal word for "medium." It's Starbucks's word, which a good chunk of the coffee category has now adopted. This is the genius of Starbucks's category Languaging. The company's words are new, fresh, and yet familiar at the same time. The first time we hear, "venti mocha," we have an idea what that might mean— even if we've never heard it before. Starbucks would never have succeeded unless it designed its own category lexicon. No one would pay $5.00 for a regular coffee. But they do for a "grande latte."

Once again, let's look at our category leader examples:

- **Stitch Fix:** Keep the clothes you like, and return what you don't.
- **Vinebox:** If you like it, you can order a full bottle.
- **Netflix:** Stream shows on your schedule instead of planning your life around them.

The takeaway: You can't name a new, different thing the same as the old thing.

You might be saying, "Okay, great! How do I do it?"

Exercise: How to Frame, Name, and Claim a Category

Framing, naming, and claiming a category starts with being an astute observer of problems. Try answering the following questions to see what you can find.

1. Imagine you are the wealthiest person in the world. You're constantly searching for every unmet need to be met, no matter how tiny or whimsical or expensive. Think of your category, and write down every pet peeve you would pay someone to fix if money

was no object. For example, it would be awesome if you could pick up and drop off a rental car right at the curb that's stocked with your ideal beverages, snacks, and charging cords.

List five pet peeves the wealthiest person in the world might feel about your category:

➤ _____

➤ _____

➤ _____

➤ _____

➤ _____

2. Stay in character as the wealthiest person in the world. Now, pick a few celebrity personas to help you bring these pet peeves to life. (Celebrities have distinct Languaging they employ, especially when they talk in the third person.) Write down your five celebrity personas below:

➤ _____

➤ _____

➤ _____

➤ _____

➤ _____

3. Now, take one of the pet peeves from exercise one. Language that pet peeve from the perspective of each celebrity persona you wrote down in exercise two. (If you're unsure how to language it, you can ask an AI tool for help.) Keep iterating until it sounds like the celebrity, and write down your responses below:

- ➤ _____
- ➤ _____
- ➤ _____
- ➤ _____
- ➤ _____

4. Pick a few of the pet peeves from exercise three, and hone them into a short phrase (the shorter the better). It can be your legacy category with an adjective in front. It can be a clever play on words that is clear and easy to remember. Contradictory words are ideal (short marathon, liquid death, virtual reality, etc.). List five versions of this honed pet peeve from the lens of each celebrity:

- ➤ _____
- ➤ _____
- ➤ _____
- ➤ _____
- ➤ _____

5. Now, think about how you would claim the problem in the marketplace by answering the questions below. (Note: This is the first draft of your Lightning Strike marketing strategy, which you'll learn about in Law 20.)

- **Who:** What kind of Superconsumer feels this pet peeve the most intensely? Don't be afraid to be hyper-specific, as the nichier you are the better.

- **Why:** Why would that Super care so deeply about this pet peeve? Probe for the emotion behind the emotion. You can use an emotion wheel if that's helpful.

- **How:** How do you know the Super is feeling the pet peeve? What body language do you see? What compensating behaviors might emerge?
- **Where:** Where geographically is this pet peeve most intense? Be specific.
- **When:** When in the user journey is this pet peeve most intensely felt?

Answering these questions should give you clarity on the right words to put in the right mouths, in the right places, at the right time. It's your blueprint to name and frame the problem and claim the language. Once you land on unique Languaging for your category and company, the way you win (and continue to win) is by avoiding category neglect, category violence, and category death.

Now, to explain each of those pitfalls.

Category Neglect Leads to Category Violence, Which Leads to Category Death

Category neglect comes from a refusal to acknowledge which direction the wind is blowing.

Toys"R"Us was once one of the largest toy retailers in the world, with its peak profitability reaching $11.3 billion in 2000.

Seventeen years later, the toy giant declared bankruptcy. It had a debt of $5 billion, and its sales had declined by almost 20 percent over the previous year. When it began closing stores, over 33,000 people lost their jobs, marking the end of an era in the toy retail industry.

What happened?

It never occurred to Toys"R"Us to market the category instead of its brand. And of course, it missed the platform shift to the Internet. The problem of, "how do I buy my kids toys?" got a categorically different answer.

Today, Toys"R"Us serves as a reminder of category neglect.

Category neglect happens when a Category King or Queen begins to neglect its category (dismissing the niche category growing quickly before its very eyes), so it stops innovating.

As a result, a new and different company takes over the category. The legacy company either falls down the category rungs or completely fails. For example, Toys"R"Us failed due to a combination of factors, including debt, its inability to compete with online retailers, and poor management decisions.

But its contract with Amazon ultimately sealed its fate.

In 2000, Toys"R"Us signed a contract with Amazon to be its exclusive toy seller, a deal that initially brought in significant profits. However, as Amazon continued to grow and became a major competitor in the retail space, the agreement began to hurt Toys"R"Us. Amazon offered lower prices and a wider selection of toys, which drew customers away from the incumbent toy retailer. The toy company's inability to compete with Amazon's pricing and selection, coupled with its massive debt, declining sales, and failure to invest in its own e-commerce platform, led to its ultimate downfall.

Category neglect is how a company goes from $11.3 billion to bankrupt.

So, what does this mean for startups? Solopreneurs? Small businesses? S&P 500 Category Kings?

It means when a new category arises (seemingly out of nowhere), the incumbent doesn't topple over because they were unaware of the new Category Queen.

They fall because they dismissed what was happening right before their eyes. It's not ignorance. *It's arrogance* coupled with the gravitational pull of "the way it is." Because the people profiting in the present want things to stay the same.

- "Eh, Keurig and K-Cups are a fad. That will be a small niche."
- "Cloud computing is nuts. Major enterprises will never give up their data centers."
- "Amazon won't become a go-to retailer. People prefer to shop in stores instead of online."

Until the niche category becomes *the* category—and what was once new becomes old.

Category neglect doesn't come from people being stupid or lacking sufficient resources to spot the headwinds and tailwinds of the future.

It comes from a refusal to acknowledge which direction the wind is blowing.

Craft beer, *Greek* yogurt, *cloud* computing, and *single-serve* coffee were all trends that could have been spotted and addressed by Anheuser-Busch, General Mills/Yoplait, IBM, and Nestle/Nescafe five to seven years before they crossed into the mainstream. These companies collectively spend nine figures on data to better understand consumer behavior. In its heyday, Anheuser-Busch alone spent over a billion dollars on sales and marketing. And back when P&G owned Folgers, an up-and-coming executive went to his boss and told him about an interesting new coffee company out in Seattle called Starbucks. He suggested they look at acquiring them but was told, "Son, we're not in the food-service business. We build the most powerful consumer brands. We are the best marketers in the world. We've got nothing to worry about."

When this happens, incumbents (and their employees and investors) stand to lose billions in market capitalization.

All because they chose contempt over curiosity—the way it is, over the way it could be.

A Cautionary Tale of Category Neglect

Yoplait was once a Category King in the yogurt market, with a market share of approximately 17 percent and sales of $1.6 billion in 2005. However, the company struggled to keep up with the rapid growth of new players in the market, particularly Chobani. In 2007, Chobani changed the yogurt market by introducing *a new category of yogurt* that was thicker and creamier than traditional yogurt. This new "Greek yogurt" quickly gained popularity among consumers and put pressure on established brands to adapt.

- In 2017, Chobani overtook Yoplait in market share. The new Category King held 27 percent of the U.S. yogurt market, 54 percent of the Greek yogurt market, and sales of $2 billion, while Yoplait's market share had declined to 12 percent and its sales had dropped to $1.2 billion.

- Five years later, Chobani continued to dominate the yogurt market, holding 44 percent of the Greek yogurt market and 20 percent of the U.S. yogurt market and reporting sales of $1.4 billion. Yoplait's market share further declined to 9 percent with sales of $927 million.

While the battle for the yogurt Category King is ongoing, Chobani gained the upper hand because the legacy companies failed to adapt. They didn't recognize changing consumer preferences or the rise of new competitors in the market. They neglected the category, failing to keep up with the rapid pace of innovation.

This neglect left Yoplait vulnerable. And Chobani jumped on the opportunity.

Category neglect happens because the gravitational pull is too strong.

A company gets used to earning hundreds of millions, or billions, of dollars per year and thinks it can do no wrong.

The gravitational pull of building a big business takes over and prevents these well-intentioned executives and entrepreneurs from objectively observing the future taking place and capitalizing as a result. They forget that what originally made them successful was their ability to change the way "it" was to the way it is—and that, if they aren't careful, someone else can come along and change the way "it" is now.

The company becomes deeply invested in the present.

And anything that threatens the way it is now is dismissed.

The problem with contempt in business is that it's emotional. It's not objective. When you have contempt, the data can scream in your face that a niche category is growing fast—and you won't be able to hear it. You've enrolled yourself in the "best brand will always win" cult (or worse, the "best product will always win" cult) and become myopic.

But contempt is also multidimensional and manifests in ways beyond just contempt for competitors. It's often contempt for customers, like when companies cut costs by lowering quality and assuming their customers are too dumb to notice or jam them into punitive contracts to trap them into buying. It's contempt for their suppliers, forcing ever-worsening payment terms on vendors. It is a sad statement when companies invest more in their procurement departments than in their product and category innovation.

Their actions say, "I know better than you" until, all of a sudden, they're done.

Contempt weighs companies down and makes it difficult to steer their ships when life depends on it. The gravity of today's category revenue can pull company owners' eyelids shut to the possibility of a different future. So they start to neglect their category.

But what happens when other companies witness this vulnerability?

Category violence happens when other companies witness category neglect and begin to attack.

In 1984, Apple spent over $1 million on a sixty-second commercial. The commercial, which aired during the third quarter of Super Bowl XVIII, was a bold and unconventional way to challenge the dominant computer brand of the time, IBM. The ad portrayed a dystopian future where people were controlled by a single, monolithic entity. But a sledge-hammer-slinging Apple Macintosh heroine liberates them.

The ad was an instant success.

Within a hundred days, Apple sold 72,000 computers (worth $155 million) and positioned itself as an innovative brand that values individualism and freedom.

More importantly, Apple differentiated itself from IBM—the legacy Category King. As the underdog, Apple needed a way to take control of the personal computer market. So it capitalized on the cultural movement happening in technology to show consumers that Apple was the innovative, freeing future. And that IBM was a relic of the controlling, obedient past.

The ad was an act of category violence.

It propelled Apple to claim its place as the Category King. Today, Apple's market cap is $2.4 trillion. And although it ships 17 percent of all personal computers in the United States (ranked third among competitors), it controls more than 50 percent of the smartphone market.

Companies use category violence to claim control of a new category.

Any incumbent that's ignorant of category design will fall victim to it.

Just because things are the way they are right now doesn't mean they will stay that way forever. As a result, category neglect and category violence happen all the time, at increasing rates. Today, you can see these playing out in artificial intelligence.

Most people view the "AI wars" through a technology/ product lens or a search market share lens. We hear things like, "The search wars are on between OpenAI/Microsoft and Google" or "If ChatGPT takes even 10 percent of Google's share, it will hurt them."

These lenses miss a material component of what's happening.

OpenAI's ChatGPT is not "better search." It's different. It's a whole new category of technology called "answer" that's being woven into Microsoft products. This is not (as many people see it) a market share battle between two products. It's a new-category vs. an old-category battle. Search and answer are different problems and different solutions. Google sh*t themselves when ChatGPT came out. At some level, they understood answer was going to ascend above search in the value ladder in people's minds.

The meaningful devaluing of your category can become an existential threat.

Interestingly, Google is starting to fight back with product and technology. It's chasing OpenAI/Microsoft into the answer category that OpenAI/Microsoft designed, with a better "generative AI" product. Now, remember when Google's better social network "Google+" beat Category Queen Facebook in 2012?

No? Of course you don't because it didn't happen. Google+ cost $585 million to build (which ironically, is about what Rupert paid for MySpace). Then poof! Gone! More than half a billion dollars disappeared.

The question now: Is Google repeating its Google+ mistake in AI?

Time will tell. Let's see if Google category designs something different from the definition of answer that ChatGPT has delivered or adds another Google+ failure to its record. But we bet Google gets this wrong because it just made the exact same mistake in Web Hosting against Amazon AWS. The chart from *The Information*'s post, "Tail of Two Clouds: AWS's future expected revenue is climbing while Google Cloud's flatlines" demonstrates how AWS is growing much faster than Google Cloud. This post is from November 3, 2022. ChatGPT launched November 30, 2022. This leads us to suspect that Google might view itself as a technology company fighting market share battles with better products and technology. It's not positioning itself as a category-designing, technology-innovating, business-model-innovating company. If that's the case, it would be a shame.

We find it interesting that many category-dominating companies seem to forget what made them successful in the first place.

As the above chart demonstrates, Category Kings earn a disproportionate percentage of the economics as the category grows. The leader separates from the rest of the players, propelled by a magic combination of word of mouth, product experience, product virality, fear of missing out (FOMO), network effects, a data flywheel, and relentless execution. When these snap into place, modern Native Digital categories grow rapidly.

Category death is when a Category King goes out of business or loses its place as number one due to category neglect and category violence.

Most cases of category death result in a business shutting its doors.

But sometimes, it kills the entire old category and replaces it with a new one. And unless the old category finds a way to become relevant again, there's little hope of customers coming back. Let's look at a few examples:

- **Atlas maps:** The rise of digital maps and navigation systems has made traditional atlases and paper maps obsolete. The digital map category, led by Garmin and Google Maps, make it radically easier for people to navigate and find their way in real time. Which means traditional atlas maps are largely unnecessary.

- **Landline phones:** The rise of mobile phones and VoIP technology led to a decline in the use of traditional landline telephones. Smartphones are the seminal Native Digital reality (97 percent of Americans report owning a cell phone). So it's no surprise that many landline telephone companies went out of business or significantly shifted their operations to mobile technology. No category, no company.

- **Minicomputers:** Do you know why you don't have a Digital Equipment Corporation (DEC) laptop? The company was the Category King of minicomputers in the 1960s and '70s. But by the early '90s, the category went night night—and the lights went out for DEC. According to Clayton Christensen, a professor at Harvard Business School, an inflexible business model (aka, category neglect) is what took down DEC: "Digital Equipment Corp. had microprocessor technology, but its business model could not profitably sell a computer for less than $50,000. The technology trapped in a high-cost business model had no impact on the world, and in fact, the world ultimately killed Digital. But IBM Corp., with the very same processors at its disposal, set up a different business model in Florida that could make money at a $2,000 price point and 20 percent gross margins—and changed the world."

If companies don't recognize they're committing category neglect, they're bound to experience category death. However, those who see and act on the mega shifts will sail into the sunset with their Category King position intact, more money, and the ability to make a difference in the world.

To avoid category death, you have to constantly innovate and create the future. One way to do that is to create a product or service that offers new and different value. That's up next.

Part 3

The Best Product Doesn't Always Win

The people who believe the best product wins, most often lose.

There is a lie perpetuated from Silicon Valley and San Francisco, all the way to "startup alley" in New York, and everywhere in between (Los Angeles, Austin, Portland, Miami, Chicago, etc.), as well as startup hubs all over the world. The lie goes like this:

"The best product wins."

The goal of every entrepreneur, then, is to build the best product.

How? Put the incumbent of the industry you want to "disrupt" in your sights, funnel tens (or hundreds) of millions of dollars into your scope, build a "monster" product, and wipe them off the face of the earth. Show their customers how much better you are than them. And when you're done? Hire a new CEO, bump yourself up to chairman, and go on a speaking tour spreading the good word: "The best product always wins."

There's just one problem—the best product does not always win.

A product can be beautiful, stunning, complex, and brilliant, but that doesn't mean it matters.

Unfortunately, startup founders, executives, investors, and even artists like to believe "the best product wins." They think "fitting into" an existing market where there is existing demand is a much safer strategy for success. So, they follow a common path to creating a "winning" product:

- **Step 1:** Launch a minimum viable product
- **Step 2:** Chase demand and prove product-market fit
- **Step 3:** Give users the ability to invite their friends and, wa-bam, product-led growth!

This is the strategy that many startups pursue, and it's why over 90 percent of them fail. What business people fail to realize is that if the existing problem already has well-known existing Category King solutions, then another "better/faster/smarter/cheaper" solution won't make a difference. In fact, "the best product" is an ironic phrase.

"Best" in relation to... what?

Other products?

Most entrepreneurs, executives, and investors don't realize

what they're saying when they say, "The best product." These three words root their thinking to "what is" and trick them into believing their job is to *fit* their product *better* into an existing market.

No legendary company (ever, in the history of ever) created a product that fit into an existing category.

Say these three words three times, slowly: product, market, fit. *Product. Market. Fit.* Your thinking immediately starts sprinting in the direction of "what currently exists." And the reason we take issue with this lazy Languaging is because that's not how legendary products and new product categories get invented.

There was no "video doorbell" category before Ring (originally called Doorbot). In fact, many customers said at the time, "Why would I want a video camera connected to my doorbell? I already have a security system, and my doorbell works just fine."

There was no "crowdfunding" category before Kickstarter. In fact, many customers said at the time, "Why would I want to give money to someone I don't know for a product that doesn't exist yet? I can already buy products from stores and online shops."

There was no "online marketplace for handmade and vintage goods" category before Etsy. In fact, many customers said at the time, "Why would I want to buy handmade products online? I already have craft fairs and local stores to find unique items."

It's hard to invent a different future with a backward-looking lens.

To successfully differentiate yourself, you have to reject "what currently exists" and evangelize a new and different way of doing things.

Category design is a winner takes all business strategy. In our category design research, we found only 19 percent of Fortune's 100 fast-growing companies created new categories. And yet, of the cumulative prior three years, these companies captured 51 percent of the revenue growth and 80 percent of the market capitalization. Everyone else falls into the Better Trap and unknowingly is competing for the remaining 24 percent of the "existing category."

As Michael Saylor, the CEO of MicroStrategy, famously said, "Why would you sell the winner to buy the loser?"

Just like the Big Brand Lie (where people believe "the best brand always wins"), the Big Product Lie is just as prevalent in the business world. It comes from an aversion to risk. Many entrepreneurs tend to avoid taking risks, which is why they opt for fitting into an established market with existing demand. Playing it safe and fitting into an existing market might seem like a low-risk strategy, but it can also limit your potential for growth and success. You end up becoming another player in a crowded market, and your solution fails to make much impact.

To differentiate, you have to take a risk.

When you assume "the best product wins," you are making the assumption the product will find its place in the world.

Why take that chance?

If you're going to invest years (or decades) of your life building a product you believe will lead to a legendary outcome, why wouldn't you give your product the best chance for success? Why wouldn't you invest as much time, energy, and resource into framing, naming, and claiming what your product does for the world as you do building the product itself? Why assume customers are just going to "get it"?

Unfortunately, entrepreneurs do this every single day.

They design a beautiful website. They launch a demo video. Then they sit back.

"We've built an *unbeatable* product," they say. And they wait for customers to "get it" on their own. They assume their product will find its place in the world. But one of the biggest tragedies in business is when a legendary breakthrough fails to make the difference it could have because of a failure to make its place in the world.

This happens for a few reasons:

- People don't understand what problem the breakthrough solves.
- They don't understand the opportunity it creates.
- They don't know why it is different.
- They don't know how it fits into the landscape of their thinking.

When a breakthrough product dies, the world is deprived of its outcomes, benefits, and transformation—until someone else comes along and reframes the opportunity in a new and compelling way.

In reality, you have to make a place in the world for your product.

This is no different than how many founders turned to entrepreneurship because the world did not have a place for them. They looked, and they looked, and they could not "find" where they fit in. So, instead of accepting their fate as the next-best alternative, they took it upon themselves to *make* their place in the world. That place is called a category of one.

The way you get there is not by building "the best product."

To build a legendary product, build it for people.

A legendary product alone is necessary, but not sufficient.

(Please don't hear this as us pooh-poohing the importance of having a legendary product/service. We *love* category designing for truly breakthrough products. In fact, we live for it. But products don't drive growth, people do.)

- **Fans** are what make a product successful.
- **Customers** are what make a product successful.
- **Other people** are what make a product successful.

It's human nature to believe we are the main characters of the show, we are what matter, we control our fate and destiny, and we are the geniuses behind all the greatness in our lives. (We wrote about this phenomenon in our mini-book, *The "Me" Disease*.) And sure, to some degree, that is true—you are the captain of your soul. But it's a dangerous place to root your thinking.

Because the truth is, the fans make a category successful. And at any moment, the fans can take its success away. If you truly believe "the best product always wins," do you really believe:

- Company, team, and business model get zero credit?
- Naming and claiming a new and different category gets zero credit?
- Data flywheel (inside the Magic Triangle) gets zero credit?

Of course not.

To create a category-defining product, you need to prosecute all three sides of the Magic Triangle (product, company, and category) *together*. A legendary product, alone, is not sufficient. So, what's the right ratio? Does the product deserve 50 percent of the credit? And the company, team, business model, category, and data flywheel can share the remaining 50 percent? Or isn't it fair to say, at a minimum, all three sides of the Magic Triangle take equal credit?

- The product matters.
- The company and team and business model matter.
- And the category matters.

If this is the case, it's irrational to believe "the best product wins."

It's more realistic to say, "The product is of equal importance to the company, the category, and the team's ability to leverage its data flywheel to anticipate the future." They all matter. And while building legendary products is one crucial side of the Magic Triangle, it is far from the whole thing.

This is why it's important to say that myopically building "the best product" is a mistake.

We want to be very clear here: We love legendary products. And we love legendary product people who dedicate their lives to inventing, creating, designing, engineering, and operating products that change human history (in ways big and small). But the reason we love the products we do, and the reason *you* love the products you do, *is because we were taught how to value them*. We learned what the product is, does, and means for the outcomes we desire. Maybe most importantly, we learned where to place the product in our minds and in our lives. We know what it "is," in a way that's new and different from anything else we've seen before.

The reason we know its value *is because someone told us*. We didn't just "see" the product and come to that conclusion on our own. (Everything we value, we're taught to value. Everything.) Products can't speak for themselves. You have to speak for them.

To do that, you need to avoid one conventional product marketing trap.

Be Different, Not Better

Better invites a comparison. (Better than what?) Different forces a choice. (What option solves my problem?)

The majority of companies that exist compete for a category's table scraps.

At Category Pirates, we call this the Better Trap. Companies, entrepreneurs, writers, creators, and marketers fall into this trap any time they compete on features, price, and "brand." This comparison marketing drives down margins collectively, and competitors are stuck fighting for one tiny sliver of the pie.

When most people say "marketing," what they mean is the following:

"We're going to launch a product or service in an existing market category, then we're going to market why ours is better than the competition. Once the world sees that we're better, they'll stop buying from the current Category Queen and start buying from us." But when this is your business and marketing strategy, all you're doing is educating customers on who the real Category Queen is (hint: it's not you) and sending that company your marketing budget.

Category Queens capture the majority of the category's upside—not you.

This "strategy" (if we can even call it that) leads you into a never-ending competition (with all the other slumlords competing for 24 percent of the category's remaining value) over *features*. There's just one problem: Any feature that allows you to "win" will only last for a short period of time. Any feature you come up with can be copied by the Category Queen, who owns the majority of the category's value. (Remember when TikTok created the short-form social video category, then Instagram copied it with Reels?)

The unfortunate result of all this absent-minded behavior is an erosion of the category's value as a whole—and more specifically, your company's margins.

This is why category designers avoid the Better Trap at all costs.

Anytime a company makes a comparison statement, it falls into the Better Trap.

Here are some easy-to-spot examples of comparison messaging:

- Faster (faster than… what?)
- Smarter (smarter than… what?)
- Cheaper (cheaper than… what?)
- More economical (more economical than… what?)
- Most efficient (most efficient compared to… what?)

Words that end in "-er" and follow "most/more-than" statements imply comparison. Because in order for something to be faster or smarter or cheaper, something else has to exist to give it meaning. Strategy isn't about "better" vs. worse." It's not about competition. Strategy is about finding ways to be different, which is not the same as, "We do this one feature 'better' than our competitors, and that's what makes us different."

Category designers focus on creating a *different* future. So the need to draw a product or feature comparison is irrelevant.

Even the world's most successful, most legendary marketers make this mistake.

Just look at Pepsi. For more than a hundred years, Pepsi's entire marketing strategy has been in comparison to the category king of soda: Coca-Cola. Over the past ten to twenty years, has Pepsi's "better product" marketing strategy been working?

No.

If anything, it has further reinforced the fact that

Coca-Cola is the king of the soda category. Pepsi's market share has been falling for more than a decade—which means, despite the company spending tens of millions of dollars on Super Bowl ads, these efforts haven't had any meaningful impact on dethroning Coca-Cola's leadership position.

Here are a few more examples:

- Google thought it could build a "better" social network than Facebook called Google+, which became known as a "sad, expensive failure."

- Microsoft thought it could build a "cooler" in-store experience than Apple, which resulted in $450 million in losses on the company's balance sheet.

- Juicero thought it could build a "smarter" at-home juicer than Breville, which failed despite raising $120 million in funding from Silicon Valley investors.

What's really happening in each situation is the company is making the *unconscious, unquestioned, unconsidered, undiscussed decision* to carry its brand into someone else's category. It tries to convince the world that its product is "better." It happens all the time. And it's always a disaster. But so many people have been recruited into the "better" product and "better" brand cults that this behavior will likely continue—probably for the rest of time.

Rather than falling into a never-ending comparison competition, category designers focus on creating a *different* future.

Don't Be "Better." Be Different!

The need to draw a product or feature comparison is irrelevant when you're the Category King.

Instead of having a conversation about the past, you have a conversation with your customers and investors about the future—specifically, the future potential of the category. For example, Elon Musk doesn't talk about Tesla in the context of gasoline-powered engines, American car manufacturers, and legacy brands. He talks about Tesla in the future: a world where gasoline doesn't exist and clean energy saves our planet.

So, what's the value of Tesla?

- If you valued the company through the lens of Ford's historical performance, you were probably one of the many investors who lost their shorts shorting Tesla stock.

- And if you valued the company through a category lens focused on future category potential, you were probably one of the many retail investors who became a Tesla millionaire.

Category designers, like Elon Musk, focus on creating net-new potential—and they get to enjoy the 76 percent slice of the revenue pie as a result.

You might be thinking, "I get it, but this sounds risky."

Let's talk about risk for a moment.

What's riskier? Competing in a $0 billion market you're trying to create, but doing so successfully means setting yourself up to earn 76 percent of the total value created?

Or competing in a $1 billion market or a $10 billion market with a "better" strategy, which by definition means, at most, *even if you win it all,* the share you can expect is 24 percent?

If you are truly risk averse, the less risky strategy is to be a category designer and create *that which does not yet exist.*

However, a large part of this is rooted in self-awareness and being brutally honest about who you are and your intentions in business. Are you a mercenary, trying to take what you feel is yours, run out the clock, and hope you're not the last one out the door? Or are you a missionary, passionate about changing the world in some meaningful way (big or small) and willing to go on that journey regardless of whether or not people understand or accept you right away, give you validation and approval, or promise you a comfortable salary with a modest retirement account?

If you're the latter, you have the capacity to be different.

Exercise: Be Different, Not Better

You can use the eight category levers as a starting point. If you haven't read our mini-book, *The 8 Category Levers,* we recommend reading it to learn more about how to differentiate your category and company. In the meantime, here's a quick overview of the levers:

1. Radically different benefit
2. Radically different brand
3. Radically different experience

4. Radically different price

5. Radically different manufacturing

6. Radically different distribution

7. Radically different marketing

8. Radically different profit model

1. You don't need to differentiate or innovate on all eight levers, all at once. You just need to have at least one on the product/offer side (benefit, brand, experience, or price) and at least one on the business-model side (manufacturing, distribution, marketing, or profit model). Pick two from each side to ideate on, and write them below:

Product Lever #1

_____

Product Lever #2

_____

Business-Model Lever #1

_____

Business-Model Lever #2

_____

2. Now, think about what your company stands for in each of these four areas. Then, take it to the extreme by an order of magnitude. For example, if your pricing strategy is to be 5 percent off the market leader, what if you were to offer 50 percent off? If you outsource your distribution, what if you outsource your sales as well?

Take each lever to the limit, and write down what comes to mind:

Product Lever #1

_____

Product Lever #2

_____

Business-Model Lever #1

_____

Business-Model Lever #2

_____

3. In the TV show *Seinfeld*, there's an episode where the character George Costanza realizes his every instinct is wrong. So, he decides to do the opposite of his instincts. In this step, channel your inner George for each lever you picked.

   If you offer a low price, ask yourself what would happen if you offered a super-premium price? If you are a food company that offers convenience, ask yourself what would happen if you offered taste and indulgence. If you outsource manufacturing, ask what would happen if you vertically integrated?

   Product Lever #1

   _____

   Product Lever #2

   _____

   Business-Model Lever #1

   _____

   Business-Model Lever #2

   _____

4. Now, think of a company you greatly admire. Like many great companies (Apple, Disney, FedEx, etc.), it is probably famous for very specific core competencies or its culture. Think of how this company is different. Then imagine that it acquired your company. If Disney bought you, for example, how would it "Disney-ify" your company for each of the four levers?

Product Lever #1

_____

Product Lever #2

_____

Business-Model Lever #1

_____

Business-Model Lever #2

_____

5. You now have a wide playground of ideas for the four levers you chose. Which ideas are you the most excited about? Which ones are truly game-changing and unique for your category? Which ones could you actually see yourself doing?

Write down the idea you're most excited about, why you're excited about it, and what a potential test-and-learn strategy could be to execute and pilot this new strategy.

Idea:

_____

Why:

_____

Game-Changing Because:

_____

Unique Because:

_____

Feasible Because:

_____

Test and Learn:

_____

Better is the gateway drug to becoming a commodity. Oftentimes, people say they want to be better. They say they want to live a life of purpose. In reality, they're just trying to be "better" than the next person. And they end up spending their whole lives fighting for one tiny sliver of the remaining 24 percent of the pie.

Once you understand that, you're ready to find ways to bring people together and create demand.

We'll show you how in the next chapter.

Law #12

Create Net-New Demand, Don't Fight Over Existing Demand

The people who know how to create demand become the most in demand.

Most businesses fight for demand.

There is no finer example than the $80-billion-dollar industry dedicated to search engine optimization. Here, companies and solopreneurs compete for the same handful of keywords and search terms, hoping to convince customers to click and purchase from them instead of one of their competitors. This is akin to kids jumping up and down, yelling, "Pick me! Pick me!"

From early in life, we're taught to compete in a preexisting game of comparison designed by someone else.

In doing so, we unconsciously submit to someone else's rules.

In business, this seems smart. Buy Google Ads for the keywords that indicate someone is already shopping and yell, "Pick me! Pick me!" The unquestioned rationale is: demand exists, and if our business can tap into that existing demand, we will find customers—and customers lead to profits.

There's just one problem.

Businesses that compete for demand fall into product comparison conversations, often in categories with existing leaders. The founders, investors, and well-educated executives who champion this business strategy believe they are doing the smart thing, de-risking their efforts by bringing an improvement to a proven market.

These people are not category designers.

When you are the creator and designer of the category, you are Queen/King—and the industry or market you create becomes your kingdom. You write the rules. You define its measures for success. And most importantly, you benefit the most from the category's growth.

You "win."

Consider the following situations:

- 1997: zero demand for cloud computing services
- 1998: zero demand for athleisure
- 2007: zero demand for enterprise AI
- 2009: zero demand for crypto
- 2021: zero demand for drone home delivery

What changed?

Entrepreneurs, creators, and business owners had to *create demand* and move the world *from* the way it was *to* a new and different way. "I didn't know that was a thing!" people say when presented with a new and different product/ service/offering. Translation: *"I didn't know that was a category."* That's because, up until that moment, it wasn't.

Someone had to create it.

Category Designers Don't Fight Over Existing Demand. They Create Net-New Demand.

In business, the unquestioned rationale is demand exists. And if our business can tap into that existing demand, we will find customers—and customers lead to profits.

But what is "demand" really about?

Demand is fighting over scarce resources: land, oil, gold, water. It's a scarcity mindset played out. And the reality is, only idiots fight over scarce resources. Think about it: Apple stores are not jammed with customers because "demand for technology retail is on the rise." If that were true, Microsoft stores would be jammed too. Demand does not just happen.

It gets *created*.

Legendary entrepreneurs, creators, and leaders find ways to create net-new resources for everyone.

Instead of acting like a bunch of monkeys on an island fighting over bananas, they work to grow enough banana trees for everyone—and then some. This is no different than how the NFT (non-fungible token) boom didn't "disrupt" the legacy art world but created a radically new and different world of art. Much of this net-new world is populated with consumers who previously (a) didn't own "professional art," (b) weren't interested in collecting or learning about art, and (c) couldn't afford to step foot in the category, even if they wanted to.

NFTs are not taking market share *away* from Sotheby's—they're creating net-new category potential in a new category of collectibles.

Once you begin creating net-new demand, the next step is to take a No Ocean Strategy approach to unit economics. The No Ocean Strategy is where you take someone who says, "Never in a million years would I ever be interested in doing a thing like that," and you convert them into your category. You turn them into Superconsumers of the new and different. As a result, you change which way the wind blows.

You do this by inventing *something that did not exist before* you came along and made it so.

For example, how do you get someone to buy an NFT more than one time?

You make it so they're not buying the NFT—they're buying

an item, a product, or access to some feature connected to the NFT. For example, the NFT collection Bored Ape Yacht Club didn't "discover" a way to sell more art to art collectors. They invented net-new "demand" for net-new consumers, resulting in a net-new business model that created massive net-new value. Creation, not discovery.

The entrepreneurs, dreamers, and innovators who've made the biggest difference in the world and created the most economic value invented something that didn't previously exist.

But this different future requires a certain type of thinking.

A Scarcity Mindset vs. an Abundance Mindset

Just like product-market fit, minimum viable product, and other poorly languaged, ill-conceived ideas, blue ocean "strategy" jams entrepreneurs, executives, and creators into thinking they're tasked with looking for a piece of geography they can grab before anyone else.

It's rooted in a scarcity mindset—and your job is to "get there" before anyone else does.

This is so hard for legacy players to understand because, when you have a vested interest in monetizing the past and present, you develop a myopic view of the future. You aren't able to "imagine the possible," because what you're looking for is validating information that mirrors your current position and the foothold in the world that you currently understand. As a result, you aren't able to see *invalidating information*—just like how the hotel industry thought Airbnb was "some little startup" and major gaming companies thought Candy Crush and casual gamers were "not worth the effort."

The same can be said for the word *disrupt*.

The business world's obsession with the word *disruption* has done a great disservice to entrepreneurs, executives, creators, and investors. It has trained a generation (or two) of brilliant minds to think that the way you build a company of consequence is by taking the industry that currently exists and *disrupting* it. You go in and make a crack in the pavement. And the result of your actions is that whatever came before you comes crumbling down.

When you're disrupting, you're tearing down the old thing—not creating a new thing.

Now, as Pirates, we do enjoy upsetting the way it is. But... *and it's a big but...* the mission matters. Disruption for the sake of disruption is akin to terrorism. When you're disrupting, you're making a mess. For example, Elvis Presley was not disrupting Frank Sinatra and the crooner category. He was creating rock 'n' roll. Crooners were not his point of reference. Crooners were not his scaffolding for designing a different music future.

But somehow, the business world has been duped into thinking that disruption is how you "win."

Now, can disruption happen as a result? Of course.

Netflix put Blockbuster out of business. Apple and the iPhone made Blackberry go night night. Tesla will soon be the reason many legacy car brands (and gas stations) go bankrupt. But none of these legendary category creators set out to disrupt what came before them. And in many cases, new categories don't really disrupt *anything*. Guitar players buy *both* acoustic and electric guitars. Many technology device buyers purchase smartphones, tablets, *and* personal computers. Home smart speakers (Amazon Alexa) did not disrupt or displace anything. That wasn't their raison d'être, and it certainly was not what inspired them to get started in the first place. Airbnb founders didn't sit down on day one and say to themselves, "All right, fellas, what's our plan for *disrupting* the hotel industry?"

If history has taught us anything, it's that disruption is largely unproductive.

While everyone else is fighting for a tiny slice of the category pie, legendary entrepreneurs, creators, and leaders are finding ways to bring people together to *create* net-new resources.

Exercise: Create Net-New Demand For Your Category and Company

The following questions can help you focus on creating demand:

- What existing demand are you currently fighting over in your category? How do you know that the existing demand is truly scarce and not just artificially limited?

- What are the risks and rewards of continuing to fight over existing demand vs. creating net-new demand in your category?

Risks:

_____

_____

_____

_____

Rewards:

_____

_____

_____

_____

- What is your current mindset around scarcity vs. abundance in your category? How can you shift your mindset to an abundance mindset and think about creating net-new resources for everyone?

- Who are the potential net-new consumers that could be interested in your category if you created something that did not exist before?

- What steps can you take to convert people who would never be interested in your category into Superconsumers?

- How can you leverage technology or other tools to create net-new demand in your category?

You may be thinking, "Creating demand out of thin air sounds hard and risky." You're right. So how do you capitalize on existing demand without falling into the product-comparison race to the bottom?

When You Can't Create Net-New Demand, DAM the Demand

This is a category vs category debate and involves telling the truth about the existing category and using the enemy's strengths against them.

A DAM the Demand Strategy is not a product-to-product comparison. There is no sales pitch. No shouting match or "Pick me! Pick me!" Instead, it raises an urgent thought in the customer's mind:

"I thought I wanted X, but maybe what I really need is Y."

It's in this idea, this gap between *what they thought they wanted* and *what they didn't know they needed*, where you have the opportunity to educate customers on the differences between the old category and the new one you are creating/designing. DAMing the demand is not a product-to-product comparison. It is a category vs. category debate and involves telling the truth about the existing category and using the enemy's strengths (acknowledged by them and everyone in the category) *against* them.

There is no sales pitch, no shouting match, no "Pick me! Pick me!"

Just a cool, calm, and collected education on "the gap" between what the market considers to be the best (or sometimes, the only) solution and what they should now consider a new and different way forward. And it's this truth telling that stops customers in their tracks—because beholden as they might be to the legacy category, they are also painfully aware of its limitations. Further, this truth telling permanently disables the Category Queen and all the competitors chasing "existing demand" in the old category.

You move buyers in the category *from* the old *to* the new (we call these FROTOS).

Here are the three steps to do it:

Step 1: Tell the truth about the existing category by placing a differentiating word in front.

A modification tells customers "this is different" while piquing their interest in the new, redesigned version of the existing category.

- It's not coffee. It's *cold-brew* coffee.
- It's not a toothbrush. It's an *electric* toothbrush.
- It's not AI. It's *generative AI.*
- It's not a water bottle. It's an *insulated* water bottle.
- It's not a watch. It's a *smart* watch.

New word combinations are powerful. They trigger the human mind to perk up and pay attention—meeting them where they are, interrupting their thought process, and grabbing them by the hand and walking them in a new direction.

This framework becomes even more powerful when the modifier hints at one of the most commonly accepted pain points of the legacy category.

For example, in the old world of books, pages are made of paper. They're heavy. You can only carry so many physical books in your backpack. It's a problem for readers on the go. The modification "e" (implying digital) tells customers, "The problem you are used to experiencing in the legacy category no longer exists in this new and different future." Notice how the modifier hints at the pain point without beating the customer over the head. It raises questions that spark the curiosity of the customer to learn more.

It *shows* vs. *tells.*

Notice how this modifier word is not an attempted amplification within the existing category, which is the mistake most companies make. "It's not just a watch. It's the *best* watch," a business might say, hoping the word *best* acts as a megaphone for their undifferentiated marketing. Unfortunately, this Languaging mistake ends up having the inverse effect, prompting customers to ask, "Best *in relation to what?*"

And all of a sudden, you're in a product comparison conversation again.

Finally, notice how much more difficult it would be to get a book customer's attention if you said, "You should buy this new Wabloo!" The customer has no idea what a Wabloo is—and because it requires an additional sentence (or five) of explanation to help them understand, the customer has already made the subconscious decision they don't care. They've moved on. Furthermore, because you are attempting to invent a new word instead of modifying an existing word, you are forgoing the opportunity to tap into any existing demand in the legacy category.

New categories are often named by what they're not.

Henry Ford called the first car a "horseless carriage." He used a modifier to remove the existing category's most valuable asset (there is no horse), raising the question, "Well if there's no horse, then how does it run?"

Ah, now the customer is willing to be educated!

They have entered "the gap" and are open to being moved *from* the existing category *to* the new and different category they didn't know they needed.

- No-code software

- Wireless phone
- Tubeless tires
- No-Software
- Sugar-free
- No-GMO

Anchoring to what you're not can be a powerful place to start your category design.

Step 2: Fine-tune the modifier so it highlights not an issue with the product but an issue with the fundamental business model of the legacy category.

Let's use Netflix as an example.

"Windowing," the opposite of binge-watching, was the model legacy network TV business used to release new episodes. It required viewers to revolve their schedules and lives around showtimes. But in 2013, Netflix released the entire season of *House of Cards* all at once. Wall Street was convinced this was the stupidest decision ever, since consumers could sign up, binge-watch, then cancel their subscriptions. We disagreed. In a piece for Harvard Business Review, we called it a radically generous strategy that consumers would understand and reciprocate. Netflix said fewer than 8,000 people signed up, binged, and canceled— or 0.6 percent of the 1.3 million people who signed up for a trial in January of 2013.

With "binge-watching," Netflix put the viewer at the center of its business model and drove a stake through the heart of the legacy category's business model.

Netflix *wanted* the viewer to binge as much as they want. Because the more content viewers can binge, the stickier they are to their subscription. As a result, Netflix (and in their footsteps, other streaming platforms) is incentivized to produce entire seasons and give all the episodes away at once. This is incredibly attractive to show runners who want the creative freedom to tell their stories across entire seasons, not a pilot plus a few episodes.

"Binge-watching" didn't just DAM the Demand—it put a massive wrench in the "windowing" business model.

When this is done successfully, the new and different Category Queen places the legacy category into check on the chessboard. Now, it's only a matter of time before the unraveling of the old world begins to accelerate. You can tell things are heating up when there's an all-out uproar on both sides of the chessboard. The incumbents start bellowing about how "insane" this fresh, mind-boggling reality sounds, while the bold new Category Queen and her enthusiastic followers crank up the volume, passionately preaching about all the incredible perks that come with this brand-new and totally different future.

Then, it's only a matter of time before the legacy world unravels.

Exercise: Build Your DAM the Demand Strategy

You can create your DAM the Demand Strategy by working through the following questions.

1. Start by writing down the existing category your

product/service competes in. Then, answer the following questions:

- What are the features and benefits of this category?
- Who are the major players in this category?
- What is the history of this category?
- How has this category evolved over time?
- What are the current pain points or limitations of this category?

2. You then want to think about what makes your product/service different from others in the existing category.

- What unique features or benefits does your product/service offer?
- How does your product/service solve the pain points or limitations of the existing category?
- What is your unique selling proposition (USP)?
- How does your product/service create a new category or subcategory within the existing category?

Now, it's time to get specific. Write down three to five modifier words that describe your product/service. For inspiration, you can fire up an AI tool and ask it to describe your product or service in just a few words. Or give it a list of pain points and/or challenges that your customers currently face and ask it to generate a list of synonyms or related words. Once you have a list of modifiers, reflect on the following questions:

- Why did you choose this specific modifier word?
- How does this modifier word differentiate your

product/service?

- How does this modifier word address the pain points or limitations of the existing category?
- How can you use this modifier word to position your product/service as the leader in a new category?

3. The final step is to educate your customers on the differences between the old category and your new and different category, using language that resonates with your Superconsumers.

  - How does your product/service disrupt the existing business model?
  - How does your product/service incentivize new behaviors or actions from customers?
  - How can you communicate the benefits of your new business model to customers and stakeholders?

If you need more inspiration, you can summarize your answers from steps one through three and ask an AI tool to generate content and marketing ideas that speak to the pain points of your Superconsumers. Remember: The goal is to educate people about the differences between the old category and your new category.

Step 3: Once you've DAMed the demand, educate customers on the differences between the old category and this new, different category.

DAM it, then expand it.

The way you do this is by tapping into your Superconsumers. Think of your Supers as the traffic conductors standing at the bridge from the old to the new. They're the ones wearing bright-green neon vests, waving their arms in the air, telling everyone they know about the benefits of going right instead of left. These Supers are the ones who adopt your different POV, then evangelize your new category point of view using the language you gave them. They are literally saying the old category's name with the new modifier. This is word-of-mouth marketing at its finest.

When this happens, exponential growth is unlocked.

In many cases, the total addressable market (TAM) for the new category ends up being much bigger than the TAM of the legacy category. And as the category "tips" (a term coined by legendary author, Malcolm Gladwell, in his book *The Tipping Point*), customers create the category winner. They *have to have it.*

But to win your new category in today's world, you need a specific type of offering.

If the Future Is Digital, You Want to Be in the Business of Selling Digital Air

Start your thinking in the digital world, where you can create, market, and sell "digital air" with essentially zero barriers to entry.

In 1981, American Airlines created one of the first digital currencies.

The currency program, called AAdvantage, gave customers something called "miles" for every American flight taken. These "miles" could be redeemed for free flights or upgrades, which aimed to incentivize repeat business and enhance customer loyalty. To entice customers to earn "miles," the airline began offering digital miles for every physical mile flown.

Over time, American expanded the program to include more ways customers could earn and redeem "miles" by partnering with hotels, rental car companies, and credit card issuers.

Today, these travel perks have attracted more than 115 million members to the AAdvantage program. Many of these members collect and hold on to their "miles," which amount to more than $9.3 billion in outstanding AAdvantage miles on American's balance sheet. But members also buy tens of billions of miles (at a discount) directly from the airline each year.

In 2019, the AAdvantage program brought in $5.9 billion in revenue and $3.1 billion in profit for American Airlines.

That's a 53 percent cash profit margin.

In a matter of thirty-eight years, this pioneering customer loyalty program went from zero to billions of dollars in revenue. Here are a few stats that highlight its insane success:

- **In 2020, American Airlines raked in a staggering $2.9 billion from selling miles to its partners.** This cash cow of a rewards program is a vital revenue stream for the airline. In fact, it's so lucrative that American used the AAdvantage Program as collateral for a $7.5 billion loan it took out during the COVID-19 pandemic. Take a moment to think about that: The digital currency American created in 1981 saved the company in 2020 in a very real way, as it did with many other airlines.

- **A whopping 56 percent of American Airlines' passengers belong to the rewards program.**

AAdvantage members are obsessed with collecting points, so they just can't stop chasing those sweet, sweet miles. The average member has around 125,000 points in their account, ready to be redeemed for flights, upgrades, or other perks.

- **In 2019, AAdvantage members redeemed an astonishing 6.9 million flight awards.** That's 6.9 million times someone said, "Hey, I've got enough points for a free flight, let's do this!" Customers don't just hoard points—they actually use them.

- **American Airlines created a hierarchy of membership tiers within the AAdvantage Program.** It's like an elite club where the more points you earn, the better the perks get. And guess what? People can't resist the allure. AAdvantage boasts over 50,000 members with Executive Platinum status, the program's highest tier, which gives customers premium treatment.

What's the secret sauce that makes the AAdvantage Program so successful?

It's a killer combo of a customer-centric approach, flexibility, exclusivity, and strategic partnerships that keep the cash flowing and customers coming back for more. But the underlying, Non-Obvious accomplishment is that American Airlines created something more valuable than its flights:

It created "digital air."

Digital air refers to any digital products or services that companies offer to customers.

These products and services have no physical substance and don't cost the company much (or anything) to produce. They are intangible but valuable—and customers can't get enough of them. For example, digital air can be:

- Software
- Warranties
- E-books
- Podcasts
- Digital templates
- Audiobooks
- Videos
- Online courses
- Webinars
- Digital art, photography, and music
- Video games
- Virtual reality experiences
- Online memberships and subscriptions
- Cloud storage services
- Digital communities

Companies that successfully leverage digital air can create new categories, redefine their industries, and achieve an increasing-returns business model.

To show how this works, here's how several Category Kings leverage it:

1. **Google:** Google's search engine is a prime example of digital air. This free service provides massive value to its users, and Google leverages it to collect

data about its users, which the company uses to sell targeted advertising.

2. **Amazon Kindle Store:** Amazon's e-book marketplace revolutionized the publishing industry and allowed authors to reach a global audience while generating significant revenue for the company.

3. **Udemy:** By offering a platform for experts to create and sell courses, Udemy has become a major player in the online education space and generates millions of dollars in annual revenue.

4. **Salesforce:** This CRM platform is essential for many businesses worldwide, making Salesforce one of the most successful SaaS companies with a market cap over $200 billion.

5. **Spotify:** As a leading music streaming app, Spotify has amassed millions of subscribers and revamped the traditional music distribution model.

6. **Shutterstock:** This platform offers millions of high-quality images and videos, making it a go-to resource for designers and businesses that generates hundreds of millions in annual revenue.

7. **Epic Games:** Known for Fortnite and the Unreal Engine, Epic Games is a Category King in the gaming industry that generates billions in annual revenue.

8. **Etsy:** This marketplace for handmade and unique goods has grown into a multibillion-dollar business, benefiting both individual sellers and the company.

9. **Coinbase:** As a leading cryptocurrency exchange, Coinbase has profited from the growth of digital currencies. It now has millions of users and

a valuation in the tens of billions.

10. **BetterHelp:** This online therapy platform has made mental health support more accessible, resulting in a rapidly growing user base and increased revenue.

11. **Twitch:** Acquired by Amazon, Twitch dominates the live streaming market for gaming and contributes to Amazon's ever-expanding portfolio of digital services.

As you can see, creating and selling digital air is a valuable way for companies to create new categories and redefine legacy industries. That's because traditional business models are becoming obsolete in today's native digital world. To create new and different categories, businesses need to think outside the box and create value in ways that were previously unimaginable. One way to do this is by leveraging "digital air."

That's why the AAdvantage Program isn't just a frequent flyer program—it's a masterclass in how to create immense value from something digital and intangible.

Digital Air Is a Marketing and Value-Adding Strategy

The rise of digital air offerings is blurring the lines between traditional categories.

For example, cars are more like smartphones than ever before. If you buy a Rivian, the vehicle comes with integrated software and subscription services to enhance your driving experience. In fact, Rivian assumes you have a smartphone with you at all times, so you can't buy one without a smartphone. Your phone is the key.

Let us say that again: Your smartphone is your car key.

If you approach the car at night, it turns on the lights because it detects your phone. It knows you're there. That means the lines between what's a car and what's a phone are completely blurring. On top of that, Amazon is the lead investor in Rivian. So every car comes preinstalled with Alexa. You can say, "Hey, Alexa, take me to [insert your favorite local watering hole]," and it will route you there.

Alexa is now a car.

How does this type of digital air benefit companies and customers?

The technology benefit is that customers can have a perfectly customized car because they have a perfectly customized phone. This breakthrough creates a radically different experience and a new category of vehicle, which is very exciting for up-and-coming Category Kings. If they embrace digital air and incorporate it into their offerings, they can create new and different categories that shape the future.

Companies that create digital air will provide exponential value to their customers.

Every company should have a digital air innovation group, even if the company doesn't make money explicitly from it.

That's because giving away digital air can be more cost-effective than offering physical samples or discounts, while still providing value to customers. Think back to American's loyalty program—it rewards customers with points for flying with the company. But it's not just airlines. Vehicle companies like Tesla and Rivian are offering subscription-based services that give customers instant access to new features and upgrades.

Digital air offerings create massive value for customers and provide additional revenue streams for companies.

The Increasing-Returns Business Model of Digital Air

Digital air businesses experience higher profits as they grow, with minimal incremental costs.

This is because your initial investment in creating the digital product can be scaled infinitely with few additional expenses. A great example of this is the Starbucks Rewards program. The program provides digital air in the form of "Stars" that can be redeemed for Starbucks drinks, products, and other perks. The company benefits from the increasing-returns business model because the cost of adding a new member to the rewards program is relatively low. But the revenue generated from that member can be significant.

This genius use of "digital currency" has brought in more than $2 billion for Starbucks, making its cash reserves bigger than a majority of U.S. banks.

In fact, digital air can often be the most profitable part of a business.

For instance, Delta's SkyMiles program generated over $4 billion in revenue in 2019, with a profit margin of over 70 percent. That's a powerful return for an intangible asset! This increasing-returns business model is what makes companies creating and selling digital air attractive to investors because it comes with significant growth potential and the possibility of high returns.

Companies that successfully leverage digital air can become virtually unstoppable, as they accumulate cash and position themselves as Category Kings.

Exercise: Create Your Digital Air Offerings

If you lack digital air, it's time to start figuring out how you can create and sell it. Here are ten questions to decide what types are right for your category and company:

1. What digital needs or pain points do your customers currently experience that your existing products or services do not address?

2. How can you leverage your existing knowledge, resources, and unique POV to create value-added digital products or services for your customers?

3. What digital products or services do the legacy Category King offer, and how can you differentiate yourself in a new and different market?

4. How can you use data and analytics to better understand your customers' preferences, behaviors, and needs, and tailor your digital air offerings?

5. What partnerships or collaborations can you explore to enhance your digital offerings and reach new audiences?

6. How can you seamlessly integrate digital products or services into your customers' experience without disrupting their current interactions with your company?

7. What investments in technology, infrastructure, or talent will be necessary to develop, launch, and maintain your digital offerings?

8. How can you create a pricing strategy for your digital products or services that balances value for the customer with profitability for the business?

9. What marketing strategies and channels will be most effective in promoting your digital offerings and driving customer engagement and adoption?

10. How can you measure the success of your digital products or services, and what metrics should you track to continually refine and improve our offerings?

As the world continues to shift to meet the demands of native digitals, the business of selling digital air will only become more vital and lucrative. You risk falling behind if you fail to create and share it. But you'll be leaps ahead if you leverage it as Creator Capital, especially if you follow the pricing framework we lay out in the next chapter.

Your Pricing Should Be Free or Ultra Expensive (Avoid the Middle)

If consumers always want the best, we'd all be driving Rolls Royces. — Dr. Rafi Mohammed

Most companies think about price in one of two ways.

The first way is cost plus. "What does it cost to make what we offer? What profit do we want to make? And what price can we get away with?" But this is a very self-centered way of pricing. It's an important consideration to include, but it shouldn't be what drives your pricing strategy.

The second way is benchmarking vs. competitors. This is a completely reasonable and worthwhile question to ask, but the answer tends to lead down the insane road of comparisons. If most other "competitors" price themselves at X dollars, companies assume their best path forward is to price their product or service *similarly* to X dollars.

The logic here is twofold:

- Competitors have already done the hard work of figuring out what customers are willing to pay, and you would be smart to follow in their footsteps.
- If it costs you $50 to make a product, then charging $75 or $100 "seems reasonable."

But these are the biggest mistakes you can make when pricing your product or service.

In a world where companies try to nickel and dime each other to death, "price" almost always becomes a race to the sides. You are either *expensive, luxury,* and *premium*, or you are *bulk, cheap,* and *value pack.* Anything that sits in the middle of its given category ends up feeling like something for no one.

When you price for your Superconsumers, instead of all consumers, you change the way people value what they value—and the way your product is valued.

Superconsumers Are Not Price Sensitive

Supers have emotional and aspirational connections to the products/services they love, so they are usually willing to spend more overall *and* pay a higher average price per unit.

How much?

- Photography Superconsumers have plenty of options for buying glass, but many value the quality, precision, and craftsmanship of Leica products. They are willing to pay upwards of $10,000 for a Leica camera or lens and are often collectors of Leica's limited edition models.

- Oura Ring has disrupted the traditional fitness tracking industry. Its Supers are data-driven consumers who want personalized insights into sleep, activity, and recovery. And they're willing to pay a premium for it. On top of the one-time Oura Ring cost, customers pay a monthly subscription fee for access to Oura's app and data insights.

- Holistic skincare Superconsumers are willing to pay a premium price for Aesop. This Australian skincare company provides a luxurious sensory experience and uses natural ingredients in its products, which can range from $20 for a hand soap to $250 and up for a face oil.

The point is, you want to price your products and services through the lens of your Superconsumers' wants, needs, and desires. If you are an Italian sports car fanatic, for example, and a new business came along and says, "It's like a Ferrari but only costs $60,000," you wouldn't be intrigued. You'd be insulted. On some level, you would say to yourself, "I'm used to spending far more *because I value the things I love.*"

So, ask yourself: What do my Supers find most valuable, and how much would they be willing to spend for that delight?

You'll discover they are willing to pay a premo-premium.

Price anchored to your Supers means pricing your product or service outside of the expectations of the everyday consumer.

This is how you achieve *radically different pricing*. Remember, price isn't just how much money the customer spends or the profit margin you expect to earn. Price can also be a status symbol. Price can be a differentiator. Price can be a statement about your company and product, and about the people who buy it, use it, wear it, and tell other people about it.

For example, how much would you pay for a piece of luggage?

- Would you pay $299 for two pieces of Samsonite luggage?
- Would you pay $645 for Away's aluminum luggage with a power bank?
- Or would you pay $4,850 for a monogrammed "My LV Heritage" luggage?

If you're a Superconsumer of luxury fashion, you won't think twice about the first two options. The Louis Vuitton piece is worth the price. The same thinking applies to any category—from toilets to technology.

A Simple Supers Pricing Equation

The best way to think about pricing is by using this simple equation:

Value = Benefits/Price

Price should always reflect the value (V) you are able to provide when the benefits (B) are divided by the price (P). Keep in mind, value is 100 percent perception. Nothing is "valuable" until someone teaches someone else how to value it. We get *taught* to value certain things and devalue others.

When a company can show a big difference by playing with the V = B/P equation, radical pricing has been achieved.

A few examples of this would be:

- Increasing benefits as much as possible and price enough to maintain the ratio
- Increasing benefits as much as possible but lowering price for exponential growth
- Keeping the benefits-price ratio the same but at a very different "absolute" price

The biggest misconception when it comes to pricing, however, is that "premium" or "really cheap" have to do with the price tag. They don't. Simply making your widget ten times more or less expensive than its nearest competitor doesn't mean the customer is going to see it as a premium or ultracheap product, let alone make the decision to buy.

Nothing has intrinsic value. Everything you value, you've been taught to value.

What makes a customer buy is when they feel they can receive the same benefits for a dramatically lower price or exponentially more benefits for the same or a slightly higher price—or some other variation of the equation

Value = Benefits/Price, where "value" is the outcome and "benefits" or "price" are the variables.

- More benefits at the same price
- The same benefits at a lower price
- Three times more benefits for two times the price
- 75 percent of the benefits for 50 percent lower price

In the rare situation where you can provide more benefits for an even lower price, you have a rocket ship. (If and only if your pricing strategy is in support of your category design. If your price is pegged against a competitor, you've fallen into the Better Trap.) And if you can achieve both at the same time, you become Tesla: both a "value-buy electric vehicle" and a "premium electric sports car."

Exercise: Figure Out Your Pricing

To achieve radically different pricing, you want to ask three radically different questions.

1. How much value does my category create, especially for my Superconsumers? To determine what value your product or service provides to consumers, you need to understand their willingness to pay and the benefits they get from your product or service. Start by asking:

   - What problems do customers want to solve, and how does my product or service meet that need?

   - What benefits do my customers expect from my product or service?

   - How do they perceive the value of my product or service?

- How price sensitive are they?

- How much are they willing to pay?

- What do customers like and dislike about my product or service?

You can then use this information to estimate how much customers are willing to pay for those benefits.

2. How much value is created or destroyed by the way I price, specifically "who I charge," "when I charge," "where I charge," and "why I charge"? This can help you create a more effective pricing strategy that maximizes value for both your business and your customers. Start by asking:

- How do customers rate my product or service compared to competitors?

- What pricing tactics am I currently using (e.g., bundling, discounting, promotions)? How effective are they, and are there other tactics I could be using to create more value?

- What is the long-term value of each customer, and how does this affect my pricing strategy? How can I increase customer lifetime value through pricing?

- What are the trends and developments in the market that can impact my pricing strategy? How can I use these trends to create more value?

3. Who are my Superconsumers, and what does my price say about them? You'll have a good idea of who your Supers are after working through the exercises in Laws #4 and #5.

- Who are my Superconsumers, and what are their

characteristics?

- What motivates them to buy? How do they differ from my other customers?
- What factors influence their purchasing decisions?
- How frequently do they buy from me, and how much do they spend on average?
- How loyal are they, and how likely are they to refer others to my business?
- How do they interact with my product or service?
- Based on my analysis, what is the optimal pricing strategy for my Superconsumers?
- How can I leverage their loyalty and willingness to pay to maximize my revenue and profitability?

After working through these prompts, you'll better understand the value created or destroyed by your pricing strategy and identify areas for improvement. That's a massive accomplishment. But finding the perfect price for your Superconsumers is only one step on the path to exponential success.

Next, let's talk about how your products or services fit into the final side of the Magic Triangle—your company.

Part 4

The Best Business Model Doesn't Always Win

Legendary entrepreneurs and innovators design new categories for their breakthrough products and business models to live within.

To become a Category King, you can't just design a breakthrough product. You also have to innovate the business model to separate yourself from any direct competition. That means how you make your money is different from how other people make their money. And if your business model works when your customer wins, all the better.

Maybe the most legendary example of all time here is Salesforce in the early 2000s choosing to sell "rented software in the cloud" in the digital world while other companies were selling "on-premise" in the analog world.

Unfortunately, business-model innovation is often

deprioritized behind product innovation.

Salesforce also had a major feature deficiency compared to the Category King of customer relationship management (CRM), Siebel. Think about that for a second. Salesforce's differentiation was a functionally inferior product with a different delivery model and a different pricing model.

But the truth is, a radically different business model can quickly crown new Category Kings/Queens. An innovative business model can be just as powerful as a product innovation. Company design is one side of the Magic Triangle—and it can have as much of an impact as product design and category design.

For example, consider how these Category Kings changed the business model:

- **Zipcar** introduced a car-sharing service that allows people to rent vehicles on an hourly basis vs. the traditional car rental industry that charges by the day.

- **Warby Parker** allowed customers to try on prescription eyeglasses at home and purchase them at a lower cost than traditional eyewear retailers.

- **Spotify** offered a subscription-based streaming service with millions of songs available on-demand, allowing access to music without purchasing individual tracks or albums.

When company design is done successfully, the new Category Queen places the legacy category in "check" on the chessboard.

But much like the Big Product Lie that says, "The best product always wins," a radically new business model alone isn't enough. A company has to prosecute all *three* sides of the Magic Triangle to become a Category King. So how does a new category get delivered to the customer—both through a breakthrough product/service/offer, but also through a breakthrough business model?

Let's look at an example from Apple.

In 2001, Apple launched a new software program that served as a media player, media library, mobile device management, and client app. This all-in-one program let people manage their Apple devices and download a "library" of albums and individual songs to their devices. It was an entirely new business model no one had seen before. And it completely changed the way we buy and consume media.

Apple called it iTunes.

Although iTunes launched with only 200,000 songs, the iTunes Music Store sold one million songs in its first week.

Over the next decade, iTunes propelled Apple into the music business—and helped sell millions of its iPods to on-the-go listeners. People could carry thousands of songs in their pockets. And they could buy new albums with the click of a button. By 2007, the iPod and iTunes had become such a force in the music industry, Apple *changed the business model.*

That year, Apple launched the subscription service iTunes Plus, which offered music free of digital rights management

(DRM) protection—the legacy practice for music copyrights. DRM lets music publishers and distributors control how people download and share files. With iTunes, you could play the music you had previously bought on your iPhone on your Mac. But by 2019, the rise of streaming platforms like Spotify and Pandora (and a healthy dose of category neglect by Apple) contributed to iTunes's downfall. But its revolutionary business model paved the way for these platforms to create a new business model: music streaming.

At its peak in 2010, iTunes accounted for nearly 69 percent of U.S. digital-music sales. Later the following year, Steve Jobs passed away on October 5, 2011. It's easy to understand that would have been a very difficult time. No matter, Apple taking its eye off the category ball helped open the door for music streaming and the new music Category King, Spotify.

The best business model doesn't always keep winning. Business models have to be innovated upon too.

Business-model innovation is happening right before our eyes in the AI category, especially between OpenAI and Google. But OpenAI is radically differentiated because it has paying customers and Google does not have paying customers. Google is ad supported. Nothing says you're delivering value like the end customer paying you a valuable currency.

The key is to approach the business with a missionary mindset.

Mercenaries look to maximize money and seek to monetize and exploit "today." Missionaries, on the other hand, see the future category as a land wherein "everyone wins."

They strive to create something completely new that unlocks abundance for all parties involved: customers, employees, and investors. So they look to make money in fundamentally different ways than other businesses in their industry. They innovate in the gaps between where the category is and where it should be and add value in places others have failed to notice.

Taking this approach, in combination with product design and category design, allows you to separate yourself further and further from any and all competition. It creates the perception of being new, different, and irreplaceable.

Here's how to figure out if you're a mercenary or a missionary founder.

Step 1: Ask yourself if you're creating an innovative business model.

This is a good way to tell:

- Do you make money when *good things* happen to your customers/consumers/users?
- Or do you make money when *bad things* happen to your customers/consumers/users?

For example, when you overdraw your bank account and Bank of America or Wells Fargo charges you for that mistake, the company is making money when bad things happen. Very little innovation is happening in that business model—and it reveals an exploitable vulnerability in this legacy category.

Meanwhile, Ally Bank permanently ended overdraft fees on all accounts.

The reasoning? It wanted to keep people from falling behind financially. (Radically new, and generous, business model!) This not only helps people who are financially vulnerable (95 percent of consumers who paid overdraft fees in 2020 are a part of this category), but it avoids the legacy business model of making money from bad things happening to customers. On top of no overdraft fees, Ally also has no minimum balance requirements, no monthly maintenance fees, no automated clearing house transfer fee, and a large no-fee ATM network.

There is a lot of innovation happening in banking, which makes it an exciting, emerging business model for the category. Other categories, like the airline industry and its excessive fees, could learn a ton from the banking industry about how to innovate its business model.

Step 2: Highlight the fundamental issues with the legacy business model.

By eliminating common fees, Ally put the customer at the center of its business model—driving a stake through the heart of banking's legacy business model. It was only a matter of time before the unraveling of the old world began to accelerate. Since then, several big banks have eliminated overdraft fees:

- Bank of America
- BMO
- Capital One
- Citibank
- And more

You'll know your new company design is working when an uprising happens on both sides of the chessboard: The incumbents start shouting about how "crazy" this new and different reality sounds, while the new Category Queen and all her evangelists chant louder and louder about the benefits that come with this new and different future. When this happens, you're just starting to DAM the Demand.

Exercise: Innovate Your Business Model

Here's a four-question exercise you can use to think through the business model for your own company and category.

1. Think about your current business model. How does it differ from the business models of your direct competitors? Are there any areas where you could innovate your business model to create a competitive advantage?

2. Consider the customer experience of your current business model. Are there any areas where you could improve the experience? How would these improvements impact your business?

3. Think about global trends that could significantly impact businesses over the next year to fifteen years. How do you see business models evolving as a result? How can you innovate your business model to stay ahead of these trends?

4. Finally, consider the impact of your business model on the category as a whole. How does your business model shape the way customers think about the category? Are there any changes you could make to

your business model to help shape the category in a positive way?

Once you choose a business model, your goal is to educate customers on the differences between the old way of doing business within the category and the new way of doing business within the new category. (Remember: If you have no category, you have no meaningful company.) What you choose, and how you choose to share it with the world, will have a massive impact on your company, category, and customers.

Let us explain why.

Law #17

Mercenaries Capture Value, Missionaries Create Value

Building an audience is easier when you stop trying to grow and start trying to make a difference.

We're going to force you to look in the mirror and reflect on three very important questions:

- Do you fight over old things or create new things?
- Do you capture value or create it?
- Are you a mercenary or a missionary?

Let us explain why your answers matter to the world.

Missionaries vs. Mercenaries

Every entrepreneur, executive, creator, marketer, and

investor falls into one of two categories: mercenary or missionary.

Mercenaries:

- Fight over old things
- Have secrets, and build in stealth
- Fight over market share
- Capture value

Mercenaries seek to protect their every advantage because, on some level, they understand they are playing a game of stealing resources, not creating net-new resources.

Missionaries:

- Create new things
- Have no secrets when it comes to their vision for the world
- Believe their mission is greater than market capitalization
- Stand in the new and different future they want to create

If you are a missionary, the future happens *because* of you. You created it. You birthed it. And because you created it and you educated others on the importance of it, you *changed the world.*

This distinction matters for one major, world-changing reason.

Mercenaries Capture Value.
Missionaries Create Value.

Missionaries serve a higher purpose that usually has to do with creating abundance for people in the world who were previously ignored, forgotten, misunderstood, or improperly valued.

- eBay values your "junk" properly.
- YouTube values your opinions and ability to entertain and teach regardless of your "actual celebrity" or credentials.
- Airbnb and Uber value the trapped value in your home and car.
- Zillow measures the value of your home.
- Fiverr values your skills as a freelancer.
- Substack creates equal opportunity for anyone who writes to capture the value of their work.

All of these companies help billions of people recognize they are far more valuable (and have access to far more value) than just what the world says they are valued at. They help billions realize one person's trash is another's treasure and reveal the abundance where many others before them only saw scarcity.

Missionaries make all the difference in the world.

To truly be a missionary, your pursuit has to be about so much more than creating for the sake of business success and profit.

Saying "I am on a mission to change the world" is not what matters. What matters is what truth you are in service of and the lengths to which you are willing to go to educate the world about that new and different future you believe matters. So you have to ask yourself:

- Are you invested in a mission worthy of your potential?
- Does it matter enough to you to spend twenty years doing it?
- Would you consider it your life's work?
- Is it worth investing a meaningful percentage of your life into?

It's not enough to *just want* to be a missionary. And it's human nature to default to a mission where you stand at the center: You are the main character of the show, you are what happens, you and your "brand" are why people should care, etc. The key is to find something *else* (other than yourself and your personal wants and needs) to be on mission *for*.

Lives worth living and businesses worth building are in service of others.

Here are three ways missionaries prioritize others before themselves:

1. Celebrate greatness and beauty.

Being a missionary means celebrating, evangelizing, and sharing greatness and beauty because of what you believe it can do for others.

- **TOMS** founder, Blake Mycoskie, found beauty in Argentina's national shoe, the alpargata. He used the design as inspiration to build the cornerstone buy-one-give-one startup by sharing that beauty with people all over the world.

- **Cirque Du Soleil** celebrates amazing street performers, former Olympians, and other extraordinarily talented people by providing them an audience (and an income) worthy of their talents.

- **HydraFacial** rewards talented estheticians who don't have a medical degree but who consumers actually trust as much (if not more) to know how to care for their skin. HydraFacial gives these estheticians the tools to deliver amazing outcomes that delight their clients but increase the estheticians' income at the same time.

- **Patagonia** founder, Yvon Chouinard, is on a mission to help preserve the natural world. The outdoor gear and clothing company focuses on celebrating the beauty of nature and encouraging people to enjoy and preserve it. Patagonia supports various environmental causes and dedicates a portion of its revenue to grassroots environmental organizations.

In September 2022, Chouinard made the radical decision to give Patagonia to the planet. He transferred his family's ownership of the company to two new entities: the Patagonia Purpose Trust and the Holdfast Collective. The Patagonia Purpose Trust is a nonprofit organization that will use the company's profits to fight climate change and protect the environment. The Holdfast Collective is a nonprofit organization that will support the work of the Patagonia Purpose Trust.

Chouinard's decision to give away Patagonia is a powerful example of how business can be used to make a difference in the world. He built and ran Patagonia *for* the mission and ultimately gave it *to* the mission.

It's worth noting that these types of companies can achieve long-term success and sustainability because they focus on more than just profits. They prioritize purpose and profits.

2. Let customers choose.

Missionaries always tilt in the direction of radical generosity toward customers.

For example, between 1997 and 2017, Keurig unlocked billions in value by providing consumers with an amazing bundle of consistency, speed, and variety. But behind that bundle was the amazing observation that in a multi-coffee-drinking household or workplace, someone was compromising the ideal type of coffee they loved, shackled as they were by a single coffee pot.

In order to truly "be on a mission" to solve people's lack of choice when it came to drinking a personalized cup of coffee, Keurig needed to decide whether it was going to be radically generous with customers and let them drink any brand of coffee from their Keurig (even "frenemies" like Starbucks) or wall off the garden. Most fake-missionary companies would have chosen the latter (saying they're "on a mission" in the press but, when push comes to shove, forcing customers into a corner). Keurig did not.

Guess what happened?

Not long after Keurig opened its arms and welcomed all

the coffee brands into its ecosystem, competitors started springing up left and right. In 2012, Starbucks even launched its own single-serve brewing system, Verismo. A columnist at Eater (at the time) summarized the root of the decision perfectly: "Starbucks previously had a single-cup deal with Green Mountain Coffee Roasters [and Keurig], *but that was just for the cups and not the machines themselves.*" This is the epitome of what it means to let a wolf into the hen house.

In the announcement press release, famed Starbucks founder Howard Shultz (who, at one point, was in fact a true missionary of the coffee category), tried to mask this mercenary move by saying, "The premium single-cup segment is the fastest-growing business within the global coffee industry. We have long believed that the biggest prize within the segment is a high-pressure system that would give us the opportunity to deliver Starbucks-quality espresso beverages at home and at work for customers who desire the Starbucks espresso experience outside of our stores."

Translation: *Shit-shit-shit-shit-shit, Keurig is on fire. Quick! Launch a copycat product. Then tell Maggie over in PR that we've "always believed this to be the future of coffee" and uh, uh, this is for everyone who loves the Starbucks brand!*

The result?

Less than a year later, the Verismo machine was deemed a failure. Few Starbucks stores carried the home brewing system, and much more shelf space was dedicated to the Starbucks K-Cup—which worked inside the Keurig system.

This is the power of radical generosity when you are a true missionary.

3. See the true value and abundance in life.

Missionary companies help reveal the abundance where others only see scarcity.

To truly be a missionary, your pursuit has to be about so much more than just "finding" competition-free pockets of ocean, or even creating net-new ocean for the sake of business success and profit. Missionaries serve a higher purpose, and that higher purpose usually has to do with creating abundance for people in the world who were previously ignored, forgotten, misunderstood, or improperly valued.

(Sam Altman, the CEO of OpenAI, took zero equity stake in the company. When asked why he does it, he replied, "I'm doing this because I love it.")

Once you see entrepreneurship through this lens of being a missionary, as opposed to a mercenary, it becomes very easy to separate the wheat from the chaff and see through the many falsehoods that perpetuate throughout the startup landscape, the S&P 500 world, and Wall Street. Saying the words, "We are on a mission to change the world" is not what matters.

What matters is what truth you are in service of and the lengths to which you are willing to go to educate the world on that new and different future you believe matters.

How you go about it is the next chapter.

Bake Radical Generosity into Your Business

Missionaries tilt in the direction of radical generosity toward customers.

Category designers create abundance.

Metaphorically speaking, while the rest of the world fights over bananas, category designers take it upon themselves to plant more banana trees. They subscribe to the belief that "When we all do well, we all do well," underscoring that prosperity is not a zero-sum game where one person wins and everyone else loses. Most importantly, they bring new things into the world, create new demand for new "solutions" to new or reimagined problems, and make it a priority to be generous in the process—not just to their customers, but to their employees, value-chain partners, investors, and of course, the community and society overall.

Why?

Because savvy category-defining companies (intuitively or consciously) understand that radical generosity is not only good for the world but also good for business.

In order to grow, every organization must have a strategy to win the next generation of consumers. Radical generosity is a legendary place to start.

What Is Radical Generosity in Category Design?

Radical generosity is abundance.

- It's Ben & Jerry's annual "Free Cone Day," where it gives away free ice cream cones to customers at stores worldwide.

- It's Salesforce upholding its 1-1-1 philanthropic model, which dedicates 1 percent of its equity, 1 percent of its employee time, and 1 percent of its products to charitable causes.

- It's Netflix dropping episodes of an entire season all at once so customers can binge watch them.

- It's Lil Wayne in the early 2000s, releasing dozens of mixtapes and hundreds of songs online for free.

- It's Keurig welcoming competing brands into their ecosystem so customers can drink the coffee they want, even Starbucks.

Radical generosity is a core characteristic of mission-driven category creators. Their mission lets them unlock new levels of problem-solving and creativity that most never imagine. And their pursuit has more to do with the presence of a positive than the absence of a negative (competition). So, they always tilt in the direction of radical generosity toward customers, employees, value-chain partners, investors, and of course, the community and society overall.

Legendary category designers make radical generosity a part of their business plans.

They bring new things into the world, create new demand for new "solutions" to new or reimagined problems, and make it a priority to be generous in the process.

For example, See's Candies accounts for radical generosity on their P&L, giving away one million pounds of chocolates per year for free (aka, 1/26th of their revenue). This isn't just an arbitrary decision. It's a core part of the company, the product, and the customer experience.

Southwest Airlines does the same thing.

It built the cost of no-hidden fees into its business model. It made the decision to not surprise attack the customer with sixty dollar baggage fees at the airport. Instead, the airline accounts for the cost from the very beginning—which is one of the reasons why it ranks the highest in customer satisfaction.

Being radically generous is a fixed cost, just like rent.

To practice radical generosity, we encourage you to start with this checklist.

- How can radical generosity reinforce your company's mission and POV?

- How can it turn "regular employees" or "regular consumers" into Superemployees or Superconsumers?

- How can it show the individual who receives the "gift" of radical generosity that you really understand them?

Remember, it's not just "the gift itself" that matters, but also the experience you create through radical generosity. The best gifts create memories. So how do you turn this into an experience where the gift giver and the gift receiver can make a memory together?

The key is to find *something else* (other than yourself and your personal wants and needs) to be on a mission *for*.

For example, let's say you're Salesforce.

It's not very easy to "gift" Salesforce enterprise technology to your cousin, is it? But what if it was easy to gift your cousin a free ticket to Dreamforce next year—the annual Salesforce conference? That would be great. But this is where most companies stop.

Remember, it's not just "the gift itself" that matters but also the experience you pair with the gift.

The best gifts create memories. So how do you turn this into an experience where the gift giver and the gift receiver can make a memory together? More importantly, how do you empower your employees to become "guides" who turn potential consumers into Superconsumers of your category?

If you're Salesforce, how you mobilize your 56,000 employees is you give them the ability to be the ultimate tour guide for a week. You make radical generosity part of your marketing strategy and budget, and you say, "Dear employees, this holiday season, you are allowed to gift a Dreamforce ticket to one person for free. The only rule is, they can't be someone who is already in our CRM or has already bought Salesforce products before. But here's the kicker: Whoever you give the ticket to, we will pay for you to attend the conference together, put you up in a hotel, and give you a stipend for meals to show them around the city."

All of a sudden, "a free ticket to Dreamforce" is transformed into a Salesforce-sponsored vacation. (You can imagine this becoming a tradition, and every year, siblings and cousins fight over who gets to go with you to Dreamforce Dreamland for a week.)

Of course, the buttoned-up accountants in the room are the first to squash ideas like these and say, *"We don't have the budget for something like that."*

Until you do a little napkin math and realize Salesforce spent $9.7 billion on marketing and sales in 2021. An event like this would be a rounding error for the company, and yet it could mobilize tens of thousands of employees into not only becoming more excited and passionate about where they work but transforming them into guides that introduce and educate everyday people into Superconsumers of Salesforce and the "cloud" category. (Remember: People love talking about where they travel. How much word-of-mouth marketing do you think Salesforce would generate out of a couple thousand people going on a Dreamforce vacation?)

Radical generosity is the most elegant strategy in terms of getting people to learn about and engage with your company and brand.

Gifting is the opportunity for talking and word-of-mouth marketing. If you can get gifting to happen, you can get talking to happen. If you can get talking to happen, you can mobilize the most powerful form of marketing for your category and company. (We'll share more on this in the final chapter!) This will get your data flywheel spinning and help you become known for a niche you own.

But first, you have to create a legendary marketing plan.

There Are Only Three Marketing Metrics That Matter

Marketing that's grounded in Category Design creates the economic conditions for you to win.

Modern marketing metrics are readily available and radically valuable, but marketers can get lost scuba diving in data and forget there are three strategic marketing metrics that matter most.

1. Marketing that drives revenue
2. Marketing that drives category potential
3. Marketing that drives market cap

Category Kings prioritize these metrics above all else, so here's what you need to know.

Marketing That Drives Revenue

If your marketing doesn't make the cash register sing, it ‍ ain't got that thing. Legendary businesses make legendary revenue targets. Being an entrepreneur, a founder, a CEO, or a business leader of any kind is to take 100 percent responsibility for revenue.

No revenue, no business.

Marketing that does not drive revenue is called arts and crafts.

The problem is that many people have a false perception that category design marketing takes a long time to pay off. In reality, marketing a category POV can drive revenue now when it is done well. You just have to focus on a few fundamental tactics.

- **Intentional marketing towards WOM:** When a category POV focused on a new and different problem catches the attention of Superconsumers, they tend to talk about it. Supers are word-of-mouth mega multipliers. (It is always worth repeating that WOM is, was, and always will be the greatest form of marketing.)

- **Urgency:** A category point of view that frames, names, and claims a problem that matters to customers will spark excitement and create a sense of urgency and a FOMO feeling among customers. A great POV creates a *before* and *after* feeling. And once people "get it", they can't un-get it. And once people get a problem, they need a solution—urgently.

- **Differentiation:** Different sticks. Better does not. Category design sets your company apart from the competition, making it the go-to choice for customers seeking the latest and greatest new thing. Radical differentiation leads to faster sales cycles and accelerated revenue.

- **Thought leadership:** By pioneering a new category, your brand emerges as a thought leader. As an educator, you attract early adopters and influencers who can amplify your POV and drive word of mouth (the greatest driver of more revenue).

- **Strategic partnerships:** Your category-defining offering can attract a high-value partner ecosystem eager to collaborate, which unlocks new revenue streams and growth opportunities in the short term.

Here are two powerful examples of how these strategies can come together to drive revenue.

You can be in the shirt category and fight it out with bazillions of other undifferentiated shirt brands, or you can be UNTUCKit—"the original untucked shirt." This category design makes UNTUCKit radically different and hard to beat in the untucked shirt category. And the now-term category POV-based sales pitch that drives revenue goes something like this, "If you want an *untucked shirt*, we built one that looks great. It is not like a normal shirt that makes it look like you're wearing a tent when you untuck it."

You can be any number of survey application software companies, or you can be the $11 billion market cap company Qualtrics—the "first experience management company." (In this case, surveys are a component of managing experience.) This category design elevates Qualtrics beyond its traditional survey competitors into a more strategic and valuable position in the minds of customers. And the now-term category POV-based sales pitch that drives revenue goes something like this, "If all you want to do is surveys, that's great. But if you want to measure the *true experience* your company is delivering across the board, you need experience management software."

From a tactical, drive-revenue-now perspective for a marketing and sales cycle, a category design POV like the ones above force a choice, not a comparison. When presented with a comparison, customers want to consider their options. They want to "think about it." But when presented with a powerful POV and a clear choice, customers are more compelled to act.

Do that, and you can build a revenue machine.

Everything you do must lead to revenue over time. Otherwise, you won't be around long enough to experience massive growth.

Any marketer that is not doing a tremendous amount to drive revenue now is not doing marketing—and they are running the risk of getting fired. (In fact, the number one reason why CMOs get fired is that they don't produce revenue now.) Powerfully intertwining your category, brand, product, and company in your marketing has a meaningful, near-term revenue impact.

Most people are in the incremental business. Category designers are in the exponential business. They build

category and company revenue growth over time, in a way
that a typical sales team or direct response/performance
marketing team can not. As a category designer, your job
is to produce revenue in the now term, the near term, and
the long term.

For near-term and long-term results, you want to focus on
the second marketing metric.

Marketing Drives That Category Potential

Back in 1936, the global demand for packaged concrete
was zero.

But Art and Mary Avril found themselves frustrated with
the complexities of do-it-yourself building projects, specifically concrete mixing. Construction and repair projects
were labor-intensive and time-consuming, largely due to
the burdensome task of on-site concrete mixing. So, the
average homeowner could not mix consistently good,
strong concrete.

In all problems lie potential.

Art and Mary saw the opportunity and got busy creating
the first bagged concrete. Art developed a system using a
moisture-barrier multi-wall paper bag, ensuring long shelf
life and consistent quality. The Avril's successfully marketed
their product, called SAKRETE, by emphasizing its convenience. Through partnerships and licensing, the brand
expanded across the United States and globally. The Avril's
shared mission birthed a new category and the SAKRETE
brand, which reinvented the concrete landscape. Every bag

of ready-mix today pays homage to their vision and perseverance—a powerful reminder of how profound change can arise from a simple desire to make things different.

Eighty-seven years later, SAKRETE is still the category leader of packaged concrete in the $181 billion category Art and Mary designed.

Here's another example. Before the early 2000s, there was zero demand for "no-code" or "low-code" software. As a matter of fact, the category name "no-code" sounded insane at the time. Software is code. So, WTF is no-code or low-code software? It was sort of like saying no-cola cola soda or no-bread sandwich. It didn't make sense, so there was no demand.

Since the turn of the twentieth century, dozens of new startups began evangelizing how no-code could expand the utility of complex software from a relatively small group of deeply trained engineers to a much broader group of business and creative users.

No-code software pioneers like Canva, Wix, Google App Maker, Appian, and many others have designed new categories that make it meaningfully easier for non-technical people to create new digital assets. Adobe purchased no-code/low-code design Category King Figma for $20 billion in 2022. That was fifty times the startup's revenue. Figma founder and CEO Dylan Field started the company in 2016. In six years, he created $20 billion in new value from nothing.

Adobe didn't just buy Figma's products, people, customers, and revenue.

It purchased the number one position in a fast-growing category that has massive potential for growth.

According to Gartner, the no-code and low-code platform market grew by an average of more than $1 billion per year, from about $3.5 billion in 2019 to $8 billion in 2022. It also forecasts the no-code and low-code platform market will grow almost 20 percent in 2023 to $10 billion and to $12.3 billion in 2024.

In 2023, we saw the launch of the fastest-growing new technology category and product ever with "generative AI" and OpenAI's ChatGPT, followed by Google Bard. This is the biggest mega category in tech today and maybe in business. According to GrandRiver Research, the global generative AI category is anticipated to reach $109 billion by 2030.

That is up from almost zero in 2022.

So, what is happening when this happens?

Something new is emerging—a new idea, a new way of thinking about a problem, a new framing of an opportunity—that's driven by the introduction of new technology, a new business model, and a new service or product. In reality, the product or technology is not what gets most people excited. Instead, what captures people's imagination is the potential outcome that the product and technology make possible. And this kind of potential is the spark that creates new market categories and radical new value.

When you cultivate the ability to create demand from nothing, you have one of the greatest superpowers in business. You're a category designer.

One of our favorite examples of marketing category potential is the Apple iPhone, which turned 16 years old in 2023. When the iPhone first came out, the category opportunity for smartphones with glass touch screens was zero. But today, billions of people around the planet have one. In fact, over 50 percent of homeless people in the United States of America have a smartphone. And 85 percent of Americans own a smartphone, up from just 35 percent in 2011.

All of these categories and companies held exponential potential—and yours might be sitting on the same growth opportunity. To tap into that, you have to know how to drive growth up and to the right. For that, you need a different type of marketing.

Marketing That Drives Market Cap

"There is no reason for any individual to have a computer in their home." –Kenneth Olsen, the founder of Digital Equipment Corp., in 1977, named "America's most successful entrepreneur" by Fortune in 1986

In 2022, 93 percent of US households had a computer.

According to Forbes, 92 percent of households in the US, Europe, and Japan have one or more Apple products, 64 percent have five or more Apple products, and 39 percent have 10 or more Apple products. Creating and capitalizing on that massive new category potential is what powered Apple to ultimately reach a $3 trillion valuation.

Looking back, Apple's intergalactic success can seem predictable.

But this was not the case in 1986.

Kenneth Olsen, named America's most successful entrepreneur that year, could not comprehend the massive category potential seen by Steve Wozniak and Steve Jobs. (Olsen even designed and dominated his own category, the mini-computer. He committed category neglect—one of the gravest category design sins—by refusing to acknowledge which direction the winds of the future were blowing.) In 1991, Olsen got fired from his own company. This happened just ten years after the launch of the personal computer category.

One of the most important things marketing that's grounded in category design does is help create the economic conditions for your company to win.

This includes creating new market categories and, in turn, net-new market cap.

Said in a different way: If investors think the potential growth for your company is substantial, they are more likely to bet on you. This is true for both customers and investors because customers and investors are people.

In this sense, category design marketing drives market capitalization.

At first, this may seem like a controversial or confusing statement. Why? Because the vast majority of people think market cap is a function of your numbers. They believe prior performance is the driving force of a company's valuation, so they obsess over metrics like revenue, margins, EBITDA, cash flow, and industry comps. These all matter, of course. And there are other material contributors to market cap expansion that seldom get discussed.

(For slower-to-no growth companies, their metrics drive their value. For high-growth companies or startups, potential drives their value as much as, or more than, metrics.)

For example, what explains OpenAI achieving a valuation of $29 billion before it collected a dime of revenue?

Its potential.

Investors' perception of the potential "size of the prize" (aka, category potential) is a material driver of valuation in private companies and market cap in public growth companies.

Your number one job when driving market cap for a growth company is getting people to understand the category potential.

Don Valentine (unlike almost everyone else) could see the market potential for Apple. Don is the legendary founder of Sequoia Capital. He started Sequoia in 1972 before the terms "Silicon Valley" and "venture capital" had been coined. And he has helped category design the modern technology industry.

How could he spot the potential?

"We have always focused on the market... because our objective was to build big companies. If you don't attack a big market, it's highly unlikely you'll build a big company. So, we don't spend a lot of time wondering about where people went to school, how smart they are, and all the rest of that... we're interested in their idea about the market they are after, the magnitude of the problem they are solving."

—Don Valentine, in his 2010 View From The Top
talk at Stanford Graduate School of Business

As a marketing leader, you want to communicate the massive market potential in a way that investors value the company not just on current performance, but on the future potential of the category.

To do that, you can hyper-focus on these four tactics:

1. **Use your POV to set up a stunt or fight that attracts radical interest.** There's nothing that generates word of mouth like a stunt or a fight. Consider this quote from Jeff Bezos' first annual shareholder letter for Amazon, "When forced to choose between optimizing the appearance of our GAAP accounting and maximizing the present value of future cash flows, we'll take the cash flows." From the get-go, Bezos held up a middle finger to every performance investor out there—and he has continued to do so ever since. Using this tactic often kickstarts a WOM wildfire, so the goal is to "feed the flames" to get your company's POV and category potential in front of as many people as possible.

2. **Create a sense of inevitability.** No one wants to miss the major event everyone is talking about, which is why this tactic focuses on creating a future

that people will do anything to be a part of. In the same Amazon shareholder letter mentioned above, Bezos also declares, "But this is Day 1 for the internet and, if we execute well, for Amazon.com." The "Day 1" mantra has since become an evergreen rallying cry for Amazon.

3. **Share your category size of prize.** If you want investors and consumers to take your category seriously, you need to back up your claims with Category Science. In Amazon's 2014 annual letter, Jeff Bezos wrote, "A dreamy business has at least four characteristics. Customers love it, it can grow to a very large size, it has strong returns on capital, and it's durable over time - with the potential to endure for decades. When you find one of these, you don't swipe right, you get married." Later in the letter, he waxes poetic about the three categories Amazon has created—Marketplace, Prime, and AWS—and goes into gory detail about the numbers that make potential investors salivate. This is important because no category = no marketing.

4. **Wow your audience with weird data.** If you want to draw in investors and customers, start sharing unique stats that highlight the impact, growth, and potential of your category and company in ways that are out of the ordinary. For example, Bezos was the king of weird data. His first shareholder letter in 1997 opens with, "By year-end, we had served more than 1.5 million customers, yielding 838 percent revenue growth to $147.9 million, and extended our market leadership despite aggressive competitive entry." That's quite an opening statement. And

it tells all the critics who cry 'the competition is coming' to sit down and shut up. It also gives him credibility to explain the next section titled, "It's All About the Long-Term." Here, he famously shares Amazon's intentions to invest more and deal with short-term negative cash flow to optimize the long-term upside.

Together, these four tactics can help launch your company's valuation, but only if you execute them well and in tandem with revenue and category potential marketing.

Now, let's break down how to apply this to your marketing strategy.

Legendary Marketing Plans Are About Creating a Different Future, Not Continuing the Past

When creating a new marketing plan, don't look at it through the "Do I like this?" lens.

A major problem with most marketing strategies that aim to drive revenue, category potential, and market capitalization growth is they use last year's plan as a template.

At best, a company will audit its metrics from the previous year and decide which initiatives to spend more money incrementally improving. At its worst, the CFO is the one coming up with the slogan that's going to go on the billboards the company is planning to run for its next product launch. Either way, annual marketing planning is usually about as fun and productive as getting hit with a hockey puck in the privates.

But legendary marketing plans create a different future. They do not perpetuate the past. And the most successful ones revolve around a Lightning Strike.

To move the needle on any of the three marketing metrics that matter, you must use a Lightning Strike to align and synchronize your marketing efforts.

A Lightning Strike is a crucial part of every legendary marketing strategy. It is not an effort to try to market to everybody. Instead, the goal is to create the Comic-Con for your category—physically, virtually, or in whatever way works best for you and your Superconsumers.

For example, Paramount Pictures deployed a Lightning Strike to promote its horror film, *Smile*. It hired "smilers" to show up in public places, like the *Today Show* and several Major League Baseball games, wearing bone-chilling smiles and neon t-shirts that displayed a single word— *smile*. Images and videos of the smilers quickly went viral on social media.

People reshared the posts, along with their fascination, horror, and excitement about the film using the custom (and creepy) #SmileMovie emoji.

The result: Hundreds of thousands of likes, comments, and shares across Twitter. Coverage in dozens of media outlets like *CNN*, *Entertainment Weekly*, *Collider*, and *Sports Illustrated*. And $100 million at the global box office in its first two weekends. *Smile* was the #1 movie in the US for several weeks—and it was the only horror film of 2022 to stay in this position for two weeks in a row. For a movie that reportedly cost $17 million to produce, the ROI is exponential.

This is the power of a well-executed Lightning Strike.

The 3 Pillars Of Every Great Lightning Strike

Every startup, company, and creator is playing three different types of games at the same time. The game for who frames the problem, names and claims the solution, and as a result, owns the narrative (The Information Game); the game for who is then able to most effectively "sell" that narrative at scale (The Air Game); and the game for who can best convert new players to the effort—prospect to prospect, customer to customer, consumer to consumer, and thus make the cash register sing. (The Ground Game).

Here's a quick summary of each:

1. **The Information Game:** This is what sets the strategic context, which is everything. It's the combination of ways in which you educate the world about the category you're designing, and learn from your Superconsumers (and amplify their voices) to accelerate your effectiveness both in the air and on the ground. This is more focused on POV marketing/ word of mouth than anything else.

2. **The Air Game:** In many ways, marketing is "sales at scale." Air Games are the high-level strategic marketing you do in service of the new and different category you are creating in the world, all the while positioning yourself as the leader. These efforts are more focused on demand *creation*.

3. **The Ground Game:** This is tactical marketing (often at the point of sale and heavily integrated with sales) that supports your strategic efforts when marketing the category and driving near-term revenue. (*Ca-ching, ca-ching.*) These efforts are more focused on demand capture and lead generation.

This is your marketing strategy, always and forever. (Remember: Word of mouth was, is and always will be the greatest marketing.) That said, sequencing matters, so here's a quick look at how to win each part of the game.

1. The Information Game

"Information marketing" can spread like wildfire in today's digital world.

For example, a few years ago, legendary copywriter Craig Clemens came up with an information marketing campaign that changed the world. He called it "The American Parasite" and wrote a sales letter educating the general public about a problem they did not know they had: "leaky gut."

All the biggest health nuts grabbed onto it—from medical doctors to Oprah.

This POV put "leaky gut" in the mouths of food, diet, and nutrition Superconsumers who began to educate people about the importance of defending against "leaky gut" with *probiotics*. That POV ended up selling more than $100 million worth of probiotics *in its first year.*

The Information Game is about:

- Having a differentiated POV (combined with differentiated Languaging)
- Finding a way to get that POV and new Languaging in the mouths of Superconsumers.

Do this, and it will be very hard for anyone to enter your new category without someone saying, "Oh! They're the Category King. *Everyone* knows that."

2. The Air Game

Once you have your POV and Languaging locked and loaded, and are clear about exactly who your Superconsumers are (the people most open to something new and different, and most likely to go tell other people about that new and different), it's time to "sell at scale."

This starts with understanding: what's the game you're playing, and why does it matter? (Not to you, but to the customer.) Entrepreneurs, executives, investors, and marketers often forget that the context of the game is more important than the game itself. Why does anyone care who wins? Because of what's at stake. Because of what it means to win and lose.

Context is everything.

Without a "why," no one cares about the "when," "where," "what," or "who."

When it comes to marketing your company, your products and services, or even yourself as an entrepreneur and/or creator, do not get it confused: your Air Game efforts are not about you. They are about your raison d'être, your reason for waking up every day and pounding the pavement, and the cause you believe is more important than yourself. For example:

- **Airbnb doesn't promote "Airbnb" (brand).** It promotes the "live like a local" category. And its rally cry, its reason for waking up every morning, is to help more people "live like a local," and experience the freedoms that get unlocked as a result of home-sharing. That's the POV the company is trying to sell at scale.

- **Salesforce doesn't promote "Salesforce" (brand).** It promotes "the cloud" category. Data in the cloud. Analytics in the cloud. Software management in the cloud. Customer service in the cloud. And now, collaboration in the cloud through Slack. Everything the company does is in service of the larger war, which is dependent upon businesses moving out of the old, legacy "on-premise" world, and entering the new "only software" world in the cloud.

- **OpenAI doesn't promote "ChatGPT" (brand).** It promotes the "generative AI" category. Everything it does, and everything Sam Altman does, is not about marketing the brand. It's about educating the world on the exponential new opportunities of AI.

- **UNTUCKit doesn't promote "UNTUCKit" (brand).** It promotes how lousy a regular shirt looks un-tucked and how different you'll look in a shirt purpose-built to be untucked (the company's unique

POV). To sprinkle a little extra pepper on the ball, UNTUCKit tied its brand and category to each other. (This category/brand blending increases the likelihood that your brand will be viewed as the leader and demonstrates a commitment to the mission.) Consumers think UNTUCKit must be experts in untucked shirts because they are clearly all in on the category.

The Air Game is real thought leadership—thoughts that lead to whole new ways of living, working, and playing. These efforts should be about taking your POV and selling it at scale, 24 hours per day, 7 days per week, in a way that isn't dependent upon you having individual conversations with each and every one of your potential Superconsumers. (They should be able to hear about it or discover it somewhere else, from someone else.)

Air Games can be everything from:

- Publishing a whitepaper on the future of your category (and revealing industry-leading research before anyone else).

- Holding conferences, masterminds, and events that educate customers, prospects, and partners on the future of your industry.

- One ad, run once, that changes everything. (Our friend and mentor, Rick Bennett, lays out how this works on the Follow Your Different "Marketing Assassin" podcast.)

When people understand why the game you're playing matters, they will gladly show up in droves and enlist themselves to be part of your team.

3. The Ground Game

If Air Games are about selling at scale and solidifying your future leadership position in the category, then Ground Games are all about making the cash register sing *today*.

These are the individual moves that tell consumers who is really winning (and who to cheer for). If you are a CMO, your number one job is to prove you know how to win Ground Games. If you're the CMO of a B2B company, this means filling the pipeline with leads. If you're a CMO in the B2C space, this means doing practical, tactical, cost-effective marketing that makes a difference in revenue within the first six months.

Otherwise, you're gone.

Ground Games can include:

- DAM the Demand marketing, where you intercept another category's point-of-sale and convert it to your own
- Aggregating customer testimonials from their origin story
- New product launch events, especially when beta-versions are released to Superconsumers, to try, test, tweak, and tell others

The goal of a Lightning Strike is to make it feel as though your company has "taken over" for a small window of time.

You want your community to sing your song, not make up thousands of songs on their own.

The key is to align all three Games—Information, Air, and Ground—at once. The mix matters. When a company over-rotates and disproportionately spends more marketing dollars and people hours in any one of these areas, they usually run into a problem. Either they spend too much time and money or both trying to "sell at scale" (Air Game), not realizing they don't have boots on the ground (Ground Game) to effectively convert those prospects into customers. Or they become too myopic and focused on winning each individual round (Ground Game) that they forget what cause they're aiming for in the first place (Information Game).

This is where marketing planning goes wrong.

Unfortunately, some companies are extremely myopic. *All* they do is ground games.

Pirate Christopher once met with a public tech company CEO who said, "We make sh*t, we sell sh*t, and everything else is bullsh*t." For these companies, there is very little discussion around The Information Game. The "debate the premise" agenda item doesn't exist. Everyone in the room just sort of accepts the premise, accepts that the POV for the company *is fine, has always been fine, and will go on being fine,* and accepts all they need to do is figure out whether to spend more money on Facebook ads or

Instagram ads and debate the tagline of the new product being launched at the beginning of the year

This is what makes marketing planning so "fun" (aka, horribly unproductive).

Everyone thinks they are a marketing expert.

People with no training or experience in finance rarely render their opinion about how to do accounting. People with no training or experience in product development rarely render their opinion about how to make products. But people with no training or experience in marketing almost always express their opinion about how to do marketing. We've been in more meetings than we can remember where non-marketing executives fought vigorously for their "idea." (We once knew a CTO who wanted the company's new enterprise software category to be called a "Thing Tracker.")

People tend to treat marketing just like any other form of content.

They apply the same lens to marketing that they apply to a movie, a recipe, or naming their cat: "Do I like it?" This lens is for fools (or for people naming their cats). Yet, it is the lens most used when evaluating marketing.

The correct lens is, "Does this work?"

And by "work" we mean, "Does this marketing help us design and dominate a giant category that matters?" That's the lens to evaluate marketing plans, campaigns, and executions—and just like a great CFO in respect to accounting, very few people are trained, experienced, and qualified to effectively answer that question for an organization.

When looking at a new marketing plan, don't look at it through the "Do I like this?" lens.

Look at it through the "Does this work?" lens.

As a founder, CEO, or CMO, we encourage you to incorporate a Lightning Strike strategy at the start of any marketing planning session.

Unfortunately, most founders, CEOs, and CMOs will ignore this advice entirely. And will go on debating whether or not the company should make a page for the hottest new social platform. However, if you hear what we're saying and are thinking, "You know what? These Pirates might be onto something," then we encourage you to invest a third of your resources and budget into each area of marketing: winning The Information Game, The Air Game, and The Ground Game.

Test and tweak over the quarters, and also understand that it takes six to ten years to create a category and have it tip at scale.

So if the whole world doesn't immediately understand the value of your new and different product, service, or idea in the first 30 days, don't get discouraged. (Sun Microsystems became the server platform Category King back in the dot-com era by proclaiming, "The network is the computer." It took a while for people to get their POV. But when they did, people understood the genius of it.)

Until then, you can still drive sales and generate revenue now by meeting customers where they currently are and using a DAM the Demand Strategy. When targeted at your Supers with the right Languaging, you can start creating revenue fast.

To recap:

- The Information Game: What you're saying (POV), how (Languaging), to whom (your Superconsumers)
- The Air Game: How you are taking your unique and differentiated POV and Languaging and educating your Superconsumers at scale
- The Ground Game: How you are empowering yourself, your team, and your Superconsumers to educate and enlist other potential Superconsumers to buy now and become loyal supporters of your new and different category over time

This is your marketing strategy, always and forever.

It will continue to drive growth, especially if you take the advice from the next chapter.

Simplicity Is Velocity When Used in Your Category, Your Products, and Your Languaging

Marketing needs a simple offer to a clear, specific problem. Your job is to get someone from "Huh?" to "I'm buying that" fast.

In 2013, a pair of smart glasses became available for consumer beta testing.

The glasses had impressive features, like a tiny computer screen, voice recognition, and augmented reality capabilities. But the device was a nightmare to use. It required a ton of technical know-how, which made it less appealing to the average person. On top of all that, people had major privacy concerns—the glasses could take pictures and record videos without the user's knowledge. The combination of these factors made it difficult to find a market for the device. It ultimately discontinued consumer sales in 2015.

The device, Google Glass, ended up being a total flop.

Why? It was just too damn complicated.

Oftentimes, complex products that look good on paper fail to find their footing in the real world. And it's because consumers don't want complexity or choice. They want simplicity. They want to look at a product or offering and immediately understand what value it can bring to their lives.

In Company, Product, and Category Design, Simplicity Is Velocity.

Simplicity expands category potential, which expands the total addressable market for your category. For example, the graphic design platform Canva makes it easy for you to create custom graphics. You don't need to be a trained designer to understand how to add text and brand colors to a social media banner. It takes three clicks. This simplicity attracted millions of daily users to Canva, which is why the company reached a $40 billion valuation in 2021.

When you simplify complex things, you increase the scale.

In other words, simplicity lowers the barrier to entry. It increases the number of people who can participate. In the case of Canva, the product simplifies graphic design and increases the amount of digital creativity in the world.

As a category designer, you can leverage simplicity in your category, products or offerings, and Languaging to dramatically increase your category's potential.

All you have to do is make everything easier for consumers.

The fatal assumption executives and entrepreneurs of all sizes make here is thinking that the consumer thinks about your business as much as you think about it. This is laughably false. Instead, they're thinking about their families, their jobs, their grocery list, and the thousand other things running through their minds. And that's why simplicity matters so much. It shows you understand people have a bazillion things to do—and your ding-dong-a-ma-bob makes it simple for them to decide and move on with their lives.

Let's dive into how to simplify your category, product, and Languaging.

We promise to keep it simple.

To simplify your category, look for complexity and simplify it.

Think that's too easy? Consider these category-creating companies:

- **Squarespace:** Web design and coding is complicated. Using premade website templates from Squarespace is simple.
- **Warby Parker:** Buying new glasses is expensive and complex. Ordering five pairs to try on at home from

Warby Parker is simple.

- **Instacart:** Grocery shopping is time-consuming and adds complexity to life. Having groceries delivered from Instacart is simple.

Complexity is a defensive strategy, but simplicity is an offensive strategy.

If you can create and simplify the world in a way that is incredibly useful, people will flock to your category and company. The irony is that complexity used to be a good business strategy. The only way to enter or create a category was to add complexity with more features, more flavors, more products. But that's outdated thinking. In reality, the world changes too much for companies not to be ready to pivot at a moment's notice. This is why big consumer product goods companies are losing money on depreciating manufacturing plants—they just want to sell more of the current stuff because they have so much sunk cost put into it! And that's a function of complexity.

Today, simplicity is speed.

When designing new categories, simplicity can increase your velocity for several reasons:

1. **Clarity:** Simplicity makes it easier for others to understand, communicate, and act on all sides of the Magic Triangle. This means that everyone in your company can quickly and easily understand the mission and the plan to get there. It also helps align everyone toward the same goals, which minimizes confusion and miscommunication.

2. **Focus:** Simplicity makes it easier to execute. When you have a clear and concise strategy, you and your team can focus on the top priorities. This reduces the risk of spreading resources too thin and diluting your efforts.

3. **Agility:** Simplicity allows a business to respond quickly to changes in the market. It makes it easier to adjust a strategy when necessary without causing chaos within the entire organization or missing a crucial opportunity.

4. **Super-Centricity:** Simplicity is often centered around the customer. By focusing on their needs and wants, you can simplify your offerings and create a better customer experience. This can help increase your customer loyalty, which can drive growth and revenue.

5. **Growth:** Simplicity is a core driver of growth because the more complex your business, the harder it is for you to pivot. When it's tough to pivot, it's tough to provide value to consumers. When you can't be of value, you can't grow. And when you can't grow, you can't become a Category King.

Your goal is to simplify the world in a way that is incredibly useful. So, ask yourself: What problem seems too complex for people? Then, figure out how you can simplify it.

To simplify your products and offerings, make it easy for people to "get."

What do you feel like eating right now: tacos, sushi, ice cream, donuts, or pizza?

You probably need to think about it for a second. But if we ask, "Do you want sushi?" the decision is immediately easier—you either do or you don't. It's simple, so you don't need to spend much brainpower deciding.

In business, the worst thing a customer can say is, "I need to think about that."

That really means:

- I don't understand the value.
- I don't know if this will help me.
- I don't want to give you my money.

To eliminate decision friction, simplify your products and offerings.

In the B2B world, analysts and consultants earn millions of dollars by reducing this friction. They make decisions, which might not be that complex, appear way more complex—then they offer a simple solution. Because if a company is going to spend $25 million on a project, they're often willing to drop $2 million to make sure it's the right decision. So, they have someone else do the math (literally) and present them with an easy yes/no decision.

Simplicity makes it easy for consumers to say "yes."

Simplicity makes it easy to buy your product.

Simplicity makes it easy to run your business.

This is why pricing experts recommend having three tiers: one good, one better, and one best. Any more than that, and you add too much complexity to your offerings. For example, Lomi—a smart at-home composter—has just two purchase options: Lomi Basic and Lomi. People only have two options, which makes it easy to quickly choose and make a purchase. On top of that, the device has one button. When the button is green, it's on and working. When it's red, something is wrong.

It's that simple.

If consumers hesitate to buy your product or offering, it's probably too complicated.

The big mistake many entrepreneurs, executives, and marketers make here is giving engaged Superconsumers every single feature they want. The result is a product that's not applicable to most people. (Remember: Superconsumers are 10 percent of the entire category, not necessarily 10 percent of your customers.)

This is what happened to Second Life, the original metaverse platform where users create an avatar and interact with others. It allows people to contribute to a virtual economy, connect with an online community, and have beyond-this-world experiences. Clearly, it is an incredibly powerful product—but only a select few people in the world love it.

The product is so feature rich, people barely use it.

The opposite is true for Apple, the Category King of product simplicity. Every Apple product is about ease of use, from its simple packaging to its easy-to-follow instruction manual. This means almost anyone, of any age, can get an Apple product and figure out how to start using it. (Simplicity is also a function of radical generosity. For example, one of Pirate Katrina's cousins has severe autism but has been able to use, enjoy, and learn from an iPad since she was three years old. The more people who can benefit from your product, the more value you create in the world.)

Making your product and offerings simple enough for people to understand and use is crucial for its success, so here are a few ways to go about it:

- **Talk to your Superconsumers:** You need to understand Superconsumers' needs, wants, and abilities to make sure your product is designed with them in mind. Make sure it addresses their needs and is easy to use.

- **Focus on the core features:** A common mistake many businesses make is to try to cram too many features into their products. Of course, this can be confusing and overwhelming for users (think, Google Glass). Instead, focus on the core features that are essential for your product to work effectively. The key here is to put yourself in a customer's shoes—what's intuitive for you may not be intuitive for them.

- **Run user testing:** User testing gives you feedback, which can help you identify anything that's confusing or difficult to use about your product. You can use this to make adjustments and improvements.

- **Provide good documentation and support:** This can include user manuals, tutorials, and customer service. By providing good support, you can minimize confusion and help users understand and use your product more effectively.

- **Leverage Languaging:** The language you use must be clear and concise. But most importantly, it has to show people why your product and offering is different. Drop the jargon and buzzwords—these just confuse people. Instead, use language that is easy to understand, avoids unnecessary complexity, and is sticky enough to remember.

Even if you have a simple product, you need simple Languaging to sell it.

Onto the final step.

To simplify your Languaging, use words that are easy to understand, remember, and share.

What comes to mind when you hear the word "sushirrito"?

If you thought "sushi burrito," you're exactly right. Even if you've never heard "sushirrito" before, you have an idea of what that might be—and it piques your interest. "Sushirrito" is the perfect example of simple, legendary category design Languaging.

Simplifying your language is a powerful way to make your category, company, and offering "click" with customers.

(One interesting note is that many net-new categories use portmanteaus, or two words combined together, to create a new word that stops people in their tracks. For example, the words infotainment, brunch, spork, animatronics, and motel. Some companies, like Bitmoji, use portmanteaus to create unique brand names that stand out and are easy to remember.)

New words make people stop, listen, and look.

This is precisely what you want when designing a new category!

It's even better if your new Languaging sparks a word-of-mouth wildfire. For example, Apple's "Think Different" campaign upset every English major because of its incorrect grammar. They argued it should have said "Think Differently." But this was an *intentional mistake*. Apple wanted to open people's eyes to its new and different approach to personal computers, so it used new and different Languaging to get people to stop and think different—not differently.

(Remember: thinking about thinking is the most important kind of thinking for category designers!)

You can use simple Languaging to drive home your POV.

Simple and clear language is easy to understand, remember, and share. Here's how a few Category Kings use it to convey their unique positioning:

- Walmart: "Save money, live better"
- Southwest: "The low-fare airline"
- Subway: "Eat fresh"
- Coca-Cola: "Taste the feeling"
- Workday: "Cloud HR and financials"
- UNTUCKit: "The original untucked shirt"
- Clari: "Run revenue"

When a company uses complex language or jargon, it can confuse or even alienate consumers who may not be familiar with those terms. (The banking industry is notorious for complex language.) But a simple message is more likely to be understood and remembered by customers, which can help increase category and company recognition, customer engagement, and sales.

Simple Languaging also conveys a sense of clarity and confidence to customers.

It shows you know what you stand for and are confident in charging toward your mission. Of course, this can help build trust and loyalty among customers. This is especially important in today's fast-paced world. People have shorter attention spans and are bombarded with thousands of emails, ads, and messages every day. A simple description cuts through the noise and captures your audience's attention more effectively. If your message is easy to understand and memorable, it's more likely to resonate with customers and lead to action.

As Pirate Cole says, "We have long attention spans and short consideration spans."

With simplicity, you're dealing with the consideration span.

The problem is smart people tend to make things complicated, resulting in stupid outcomes.

In reality, smart people are not as smart as they think they are. The smartest executives, investors, and leaders can act with deeper and deeper levels of precision, but this often confuses people. In fact, executives often get paid to complicate things! But complexity can be too much for the external world. Remember, people have a bazillion things going on—they don't need another clever, complicated ad campaign hitting them in the face while working through their to-do lists.

As Pirate Christopher says, "Let's not be so smart, we're stupid."

The people who disagree with the notion of simplicity is velocity are smart, but in the classic sense of being "smart." They probably went to a great school, got great scores, and landed a steady, high-paying job. But that kind of smart only requires memorization and regurgitation—the ability to store a massive amount of information in your head, sift through it, and recall it quickly.

For most companies, this amounts to being "smart" and credible.

But this type of "smart" isn't smart enough to see patterns.

It isn't smart enough to see patterns across multiple categories. And it's not smart enough to actually see the pattern behind the pattern that allows you to simplify the category, company, and offerings you want to explain to the world. The ability to memorize and regurgitate does not require the same amount of intelligence as the ability to recognize and simplify patterns.

Pattern recognition and simplification require a different kind of smart.

The reason simplicity is velocity is that it allows you to shortcut memorization and regurgitation and move on to pattern recognition and simplification. It's like the Disneyland FastPass—you cut to the front of the line, which allows you to move faster and make better decisions. You get an advantage over everyone else waiting in the line. Only then can you recognize patterns across multiple domains and see the pattern behind the pattern, which allows you to simplify everything.

This is what ultimately sparks a word-of-mouth marketing wildfire.

Law #22

When Word of Mouth Sticks, Your Category Tips

To create marketing with viral lift, you have to put the right words in the right mouths.

Word of mouth is, and will forever be, the most powerful form of marketing.

Unfortunately, the way most entrepreneurs, executives, and creators think about word of mouth is by "reaching as many people as possible, as cheaply as possible." Conventional wisdom assumes the more people who hear your message, the more people will spread your message. But this just isn't true. When this strategy fails, most marketing experts think the problem was "the creative" or the "ad buys" or any number of other traditional marketing levers. What they fail to consider is that their marketing did not create viral lift, with a decreasing customer acquisition cost, because they did not put the right words in the right mouths.

In reality, word of mouth is all about talking.

Word of mouth (WOM) is about putting the right words (POV) in the right mouths (Superconsumers) in the right places (Super-Geos).

The people who are most likely to want to talk about your product, service, platform, or category are people who are obsessed with that kind of thing.

They're Superconsumers.

A Superconsumer is the kind of person who knows your category better than anyone else—and as a result, is willing to spend 30 to 70 percent more with you than other less enthusiastic customers. The analogy we like to draw here is that if you are a Super of Pink Floyd, you don't just buy *The Dark Side of the Moon* record once. You buy it maybe a dozen times. You have the original record, a few unopened CDs, various digital copies across different devices, some live bootlegs, as well as one or two remastered versions. You've probably also bought copies to give as gifts to friends. You might even have a lunch box.

What doesn't get talked about enough is how powerful Superconsumers can be in unlocking exponential growth for your business via word-of-mouth marketing.

Superconsumers are not doing WOM marketing because you hypnotized them into it. They're talking about your product, *and more importantly, the category,* because they heard your unique POV, internalized it, tried it, experienced a transformation of some kind, and are now *over-the-moon excited* to help other people experience the same transformation they did.

But not all WOM marketing is the same. So let's walk through the five different levels:

The Five Levels of Word-of-Mouth Marketing

- **Level 1:** **If you want negative WOM, sell to the customer.** This guarantees they won't tell anyone about your product/service—and if they do, it'll likely be to complain about how you were trying (hard) to sell to them.

- **Level 2:** **If you want to open the door for WOM, create the perception that everyone else is buying.** This is what happens when you see a restaurant that's jam-packed with a line down the street. You assume it's good—because other people are buying and sticking around. So it must be awesome. (Ever experienced the inverse? You go to a restaurant, see very few people, and say, "Hmmm… no one is in there. Maybe we should eat somewhere else!" *Humans are pack animals.*)

- **Level 3:** **If you want to spark WOM, help the customer realize the benefit your product/service solves is the opposite of what they thought was possible.** In other words, "wanna hear something weird" WOM is incredibly effective at piercing through the noise. For example, how do you get someone to talk about getting a HydraFacial? You tell them that the best part of the HydraFacial is looking at the vial that collects all the dead skin, blackheads, whiteheads, and disgustingness that was just extracted from their face. The person listening thinks, "Wait a minute, why are you sharing something so disgusting? It's not like I blow my nose and excitedly show the contents of my Kleenex to you." Then they think, "Whoa! I didn't know I had all that gunk inside my face too!" This causes them to immediately need to tell their friends, "You need to get a HydraFacial! You have no idea how much dirt is hiding inside your face!"

- **Level 4: If you want WOM to catch fire and spread, help the customer understand how this thing will transform their life.** The product/service is awesome. The outcome is the opposite of what they thought. Now, let them see the future. Educate them on the bigger mission. What does their life look like after using this product/service? What does the *world* look like if tons of people start using this product/service?

- **Level 5: And if you want WOM to spread like crazy, help the customer make money.** When the product/service is awesome, and it allows them to transform and live a different future, *and* there is economic value, WOM spirals out of control.

But WOM doesn't do you any good if random people all over the world are talking about your category. What you really want is a small group of Superconsumers who live inside a (digital or analog) Super-Geo. These Supers should be evangelizing your category *such that other people in this Super-Geo can't go anywhere without hearing about it.* This gives you the illusion of being "everywhere." As a result, "the right words" keep coming out of "the right mouths," and revenue begins to accelerate exponentially as the result of proximity.

Super-Geos are portals to new dimensions—and when you find one, you suddenly "live in the future."

A Super-Geo is a specific place (analog or digital) where a group of Superconsumers is together:

- Geographically (Chicago or a suburb east of Atlanta, etc.)
- Digitally (a Discord channel, a Facebook group, a gaming chat room, etc.)
- Affinity (a neighborhood that is predominantly Catholic, Jewish, or Hindu. Or a spot where all the local surfers, artists, or bankers hang out.)
- Vocationally (a club, a fraternity, or a sorority, a shared specialized school, etc.)

These are areas of *extreme* demand density.

This is how a tiny zip code on a relative basis becomes exponentially more profitable than anywhere else you serve customers. Or how a single Facebook group, Discord channel, or email newsletter partnership can yield fifty times more ROI than any other marketing channel. What you're doing (whether you realize it or not) is tapping into a Super-Geo full of your Superconsumers—who buy more, at higher prices, more often—and bring more people to the category and your brand.

This becomes a virtuous circle, creating WOM at scale.

To discover these Super-Geo opportunities, you must put on your category scientist lens. You have to analyze data from the past *with a mindset focused on spotting the "weird"* so you can discover/create the wormholes that lead to *different* futures. This is easier said than done. Most marketers do not think about Super-Geos this way.

But when you play with this lens yourself, you'll quickly develop a new relationship with data.

How do you find Super-Geos?

The Super-Geos you are looking for are not continents or even countries.

What you are looking for is data at the state level. And not just state, but city. And not just city, but zip code. Or digitally speaking: not just the platform (LinkedIn), but a group of users on the platform (LinkedIn Group).

For example, most companies have sales data by geography.

They can see that they sell more in zip code A vs. zip code B. But what they often fail to do is *normalize* the data by converting it into a per capita metric. You can then take other per capita metrics (Super of 1 = Super of 9) and see what weirdness you can find.

Here's the detailed ten-step recipe.

Exercise: Find Your WOM Super-Geos

1. **Take your data by geography at the most granular level you can.** (State, city, DMA, zip code, zip + 4, etc.)

2. **Convert it into a per capita metric.** If you have total category consumers from a third-party source (Nielsen, IDG), then great. If not, using the total population by that geography can be good enough. Make sure you adjust it for gender, age, etc.

3. **Compare the per capita metric to year-over-year sales growth in that geography.** What do you see? Do you find that sales growth is slow on very low per capita metrics, jumps really high with moderate per capita metrics, then slows again with high per capita metrics? Congratulations, you just built yourself your category S-curve!

4. **Append your dataset to other per capita metrics, using geography as the common denominator.** Get as broad of datasets as you possibly can.

5. **Now compare the per capita metrics to other per capita metrics.** Competitors in your category. Adjacent categories. Random categories you would not think have any relationship to yours. This is your data potluck!

6. **Stare at the per capita data with a weird audience.** Experts and novices in the category. Senior executives and junior employees. Cross-functional employees and experts. Superconsumers and nonusers of the category. What two points can be connected?

7. **Even better, get longitudinal data to create a time series effect.** What goes up and down at the same time? Which ones are positively and negatively correlated?

8. **Combine that data with government data from NOAA (climate), CDC (medical/health), the Bureau of Labor Statistics, Personal Consumer Expenditure surveys, traffic data, home building data, demographic data, moving data, etc.** What do you see?

9. **Look at the local markets with the most compelling per capita metrics with clear causal factors from the wide array of data points.** Can you tell a story about it that makes sense? Those are your Super-Geos.

10. **Final step!** Take a look at the markets that have (a) all the causal factors but (b) relatively lower per capita category spending. Those are your potential Super-Geos. They have all the signs that a particular local market *should* become a Super-Geo. Now run some heavy up-marketing tests to prove whether your hypothesis is true (or not).

Congratulations! You now have the Super-Geo data to inform your Lighting Strike strategy that targets your Super-consumers and tips word of mouth in your favor. All that's left is to take everything you've learned from this book and start applying it to your own category and company.

Remember: Being a great category designer isn't about being conventional. It's about training yourself to reject the premise and to reject "what's normal." The incentives are in your favor if you're comfortable with "weird." If you can handle being called a fool in the short term, you'll be the one who looks like a genius in the long term.

You'll be the one who spots and acts on exponential opportunities. You'll be the one who earns an outsized economic reward. You'll be the one who becomes the Category King/Queen.

Now, go forth and create that new and different future!

Meet The Category Pirates

Category Pirates is the authority on category creation and category design.

Every month, our writing band publishes "mini-books" (3,000 to 8,000 words) for the radically different—who want to see, design, and dominate categories of consequence. If you are reading this book, that means you probably stumbled upon Category Pirates somewhere else, like Amazon. And while we republish our "mini-books" on other platforms, the Category Pirates paid newsletter is our first-stop destination for new category designers. There, our "mini-books" are more interactive, and we are better able to directly connect with readers like you.

Mini-book topics include:

- How to create new categories and redesign old ones.
- The Magic Triangle, The 8 Levers, The Category Design Scorecard, and dozens of frameworks for how to create and design new categories.
- Case studies for how successful companies have

successfully created and/or redesigned existing categories (and where other companies have gone wrong).

- Motivational examples of the power of creating and investing in category creators such as Tesla, Netflix, Amazon, Airbnb, and more.

Every new mini-book goes directly to your inbox.

- Free subscribers receive previews of every "mini-book" and occasional free content
- Paying subscribers get access to every "mini-book" and occasional paid-only content

You can subscribe to Category Pirates here: https://categorypirates.substack.com

If you prefer books over newsletters, you can also pick up our other Category Pirates bestsellers:

- *The Category Design Toolkit*
- *A Marketer's Guide To Category Design*
- *Snow Leopard*

But you may be wondering, who are the Category Pirates?

Meet Pirate Eddie Yoon

Eddie Yoon has written more on category strategy for Harvard Business Review than any other person.

Eddie is the founder of EddieWouldGrow, LLC, a think tank and advisory firm on growth strategy, and co-founder of Category Pirates. Previously, he was one of the senior partners at The Cambridge Group, a strategy consulting firm. His work over the past two decades has driven over $8 billion dollars of annual incremental revenue. In particular, 8 of his clients have doubled or tripled in revenue in less than 8 years. Eddie is one of the world's leading experts on finding and monetizing Superconsumers to grow and create new categories.

He is the author of the book **Superconsumers:** *A Simple, Speedy and Sustainable Path to Superior Growth* (Harvard Business School Press, 2016). His book was named as one of the Best Business Books of 2017 by Strategy & Business. Eddie is also the author of over 100 articles, including "Make Your Best Customers Even Better" (Harvard Business Review magazine, March 2014) and "Why It Pays to Be a Category Creator" (Harvard Business Review magazine, March 2013). Additionally, he has appeared on CNBC and MSNBC, and been quoted in *The Wall Street Journal, The Economist,* and *Forbes* for his predictions on future category potential of publicly traded companies, as well as been a keynote speaker at industry-leading events in the U.S., Canada, Kenya, Australia, New Zealand, Denmark, the UK, and Japan.

Eddie holds an AB in Political Science and Economics from

the University of Chicago. Born and raised in Hawaii, he went to the Punahou School in Honolulu. Today, Eddie lives in Chicago with his wife and three children.

Meet Pirate
Christopher Lochhead

Christopher Lochhead is a top 0.5% author, newsletter creator, and podcaster who is best known as a "godfather" of Category Design.

He teaches entrepreneurs, creators, and marketers to design and dominate new market categories. All of his work is co-created with friends and partners. Christopher's first two books, *Play Bigger* and *Niche Down*, were the first texts written on the management discipline of Category Design.

Christopher lives and breathes category design as an advisor to over 50 venture-backed startups, a venture capital limited partner, and a former three-time Silicon Valley public company CMO (Mercury Interactive, Scient, and Vantive). Christopher is also the host of Follow Your Different, a popular business dialogue podcast, and Lochhead on Marketing, a marketing and category design podcast. He is also a co-founder of the "business writing band" Category Pirates.

The Marketing Journal calls him "one of the best minds in marketing," NBA legend Bill Walton calls him a "quasar," The Economist calls him "off-putting to some," and some podcast reviewers think he is "overrated" and "not worth it." Podcaster Neil Pearlberg calls Follow Your Different "the worst business podcast," and Podcast Magazine calls Follow Your Different "the best business podcast."

As a dyslexic paperboy from Montreal who got thrown out of school at 18 years old, Christopher believes if you're lucky enough to make it to the top of a mountain, you should throw down a rope.

Meet Pirate Nicolas Cole

Nicolas Cole is one of the most prolific digital writers in the world.

"Cole" as he's known, is an author, viral writer, ghostwriter, and serial "writing entrepreneur." He is the co-founder of Ship 30 for 30 (a cohort-based community to help people start writing online), Digital Press (a ghostwriting agency for founders, executives, and industry leaders), and Category Pirates. He's been writing online since he was 17 years old—and to date has accumulated hundreds of millions of views on his work.

In 2015, Cole became the #1 most-read writer on Quora (a Question/Answer website with more than 300 million users). And in 2016, he was one of *Inc Magazine's* Top 10 contributing writers, bringing in millions of page views for the publication. His work has been republished all across the Internet, including: *TIME, Forbes, Fortune, Business Insider, CNBC, Harvard Business Review,* and more.

Over the years, Cole has written more than 3,000 articles online, as well as thousands more under other people's names. He has ghostwritten for hundreds of Silicon Valley founders, Fortune 500 executives, renowned venture capitalists and angel investors, Grammy-winning musicians, Olympic athletes, *New York Times* best-selling authors, and more.

Finally, Cole is the author of the best-selling book, *The Art & Business of Online Writing*, which has become a must-read in the digital publishing world.

He lives in Miami but will forever be from Chicago.

Meet Pirate Katrina Kirsch

Katrina Kirsch is the Head of Operations and Publishing for Category Pirates, and a driving force behind the scenes of the Pirate Ship. Here, she helps ideate and map out content, wrangles ideas, engages with subscribers, co-creates and publishes the mini-books, and ensures the digital wheels keep turning.

As a newly-initated category designer, Katrina is learning how to unlearn and relearning how to learn. Discovering the radically different business discipline of category design has changed the course of her career, which began in the startup tech world as an editor and a writer. She has collaborated with companies such as HubSpot, Digital Press, ThirdLove, M1, Photographers Without Borders, and of course, Category Pirates. She has spent her entire career diving into words and has brought over 573 articles, 18 mini-books, and multiple books to life. She is also the founder of Editpreneur, a digital editing agency for self-publishing business leaders.

Born and raised in Chicago, Katrina began traveling the world at the age of eighteen. After a brief battle with traditional office life in 2015, she switched to a remote work lifestyle and became known as the "crazy" one who is constantly on the move. She has since lived and worked in over eighteen countries and dozens of cities—and the list continues to grow.

No matter where she is, Katrina helps creators get their written work out into the world.

73358858R00157